Compiled by:
Brookside Publishers
420 Weaver Road
Millersburg, PA 17061

Printed in the U.S.A.

Copyright 1999
Brookside Publishers
420 Weaver Road
Millersburg, PA 17061 U.S.A.

I.S.B.N. PB
0-9670627-3-X

Forward

When a person decides to write a book about such an unusual storm of a hurricane, as the Hurricane Mitch of 1998, he will find that his task is very large and also very unusual, which I found out! What had to be done is to try and find the areas where we could contact people that could speak English and to glean stories that we felt were of interest to the general public.

To obtain this information we made contact with different newspapers and through C.A.M. and numerous other people. See page III for information on people helping us. But after you plunge into such a job you are forced to realize that one book could not hold nearly everything that could be written from the personal experiences that these people have had when this hurricane swept over them, which leaves the questions: Why do our floods become increasingly destructive? And why, during the advance of our modern technology, can we not be better prepared for a deluge like this?

It seems the more modern technology we have, the more and greater the floods and earthquakes are appearing so we need to think back to Noah's time in the Bible as it is quoted in the King James Version, *"And the Lord said, "I will destroy man whom I have created from the face of the earth; both man and beast, and the creeping thing, and the fowls of the air; for it repenteth me that I have made them."* Genesis 6:7. *"And behold I, even I, do bring a flood of waters upon the Earth…"* Genesis 6:17.

But Noah and his family found grace in the eyes of the Lord. The story of a deluge which overwhelmed the entire world, destroying most of the living creatures is one of the oldest stories in the memories, tradition and record of man.

So altogether, the job of writing a book about any one flood is an experience that after you have gotten into, it takes you farther along than you figured on when first started.

Again, if we have deleted some stories and pictures of happenings, we do not want to offend anyone, but the book just could not hold everything that we collected. We truthfully want to thank everyone for their time and effort for getting information for us and the encouragement that we got along the way.

Also, some of these pictures are not as clear as we would wish, but they will show the objects that we wanted. We had to fill in some pictures with text that was provided, but not necessarily meaning that all pictures belong with a certain story.

Elam Lapp

Dedicated

This book is dedicated to the countless people who died amid this hurricane storm called Mitch and also the countless voluntary hours spent by Christian Aid Ministries and Mennonite Central Committees and to all voluntary organizations and countries throughout the world.

We also give special thanks to all the people who have spent time to send us pictures and short stories of their experience of Hurricane Mitch. Without this effort this book would not have been possible. Listed below are the people who we made contact with.

May God bless you all in your efforts.

Elam Lapp

Special Thanks To:

David Troyer	Jorge Torres
Dan Hostetler	Jack Brown, Nica News
Dan Shetler	Tom Stargardter, Nica News
Larry Leibowitz	Dr. Mayer J. Heiman, M.D.
Ella Jean Shenk	Jennifer Hautle, Typesetter
Charlotte Shank	Amy Smith, Typesetter
David & Nancy Stutzman	Sue King, Typesetter
Jon Stoltzfus	Jermia Martin
Carl Martin	Jacob A. Bear
Ivan Ray Sensening	Max Lemus, La Prensia
Henry & Judy Leiva	Newspaper
Bob Izpedski	Ken Sensening

Pictures and Images were provided by: La Prensia Newspaper, Jorge L. Torres, Vica TV, Corporacion Televecentro, Hondused and individuals listed above.

The publisher's purpose, after defraying some of the expenses of publishing and selling this book is to devote a portion of the profits which may occur from the sale of this title and give to the people of Central America suffering from Hurricane Mitch of October and November 1998 through Christian Aid Ministries and Mennonite Central Committee.

The Publisher

Preface

MITCH
The Deadliest Atlantic Hurricane Since 1780

In an awesome display of power and destruction, with 72 inches of rain recorded, Hurricane Mitch will be remembered as the most deadly hurricane to strike the Western Hemisphere in the last two centuries! Not since the Great Hurricane of 1780, which killed approximately 22,000 people in the eastern Caribbean, was there a more deadly hurricane. Mitch struck Central America with such viciousness that it was nearly a week before the magnitude of the disaster began to reach the outside world. The death toll currently is reported as 11,000 with thousands of others missing. Though the final death toll will never be known, it is quite likely that Mitch directly killed more people than any Atlantic hurricane in over 200 years. More than three million people were either homeless or severely affected. In this extremely poor third world region of the globe, estimates of the total damage from the storm are at $5 billion and rising. The President of Honduras, Carlos Flores Facusse, claimed the storm destroyed 50 years of progress.

CATEGORY 5 STORM

Within four days of its birth as a tropical depression on October 22, 1998, Mitch had grown into a Category 5 storm on the Saffir-Simpson Hurricane Scale. By 2100 UTC on October 26, the storm had deepened to a pressure of 905 millibars with sustained winds of 155 knots (180 mph) and gusts well over 200 mph! Mitch thus became tied for the fourth strongest Atlantic hurricane on record based upon barometric pressure values. Though the pressure began rising six hours later, Mitch remained at Category 5 status for a continuous period of 33 hours - the longest continuous period for a Category 5 storm since the 36 consecutive hours by Hurricane David in 1979. In addition, Mitch maintained sustained winds of 155 knots for 15 hours, and 72" of rain - the third longest period of such winds on record after the continuous 18 hours of 155 knot winds or higher by Hurricane Camille in 1969 and Hurricane Dog in 1950. Though exact comparisons are suspect due to differing frequencies in observation times (3-hourly versus 6-hourly observations) and a bias in earlier years toward higher estimated wind speeds, it is quite apparent that Mitch was one of the stronger storms ever recorded in the Atlantic.

ASSAULT ON CENTRAL AMERICA

After threatening Jamaica and the Cayman Islands, Mitch moved westward and by 2100 UTC on October 27, the Category 5 storm was about 60 miles north of Trujilo on the north coast of Honduras. Preliminary wave height estimates north of Honduras during this time at the height of the hurricane are as high as 44 feet, according to one wave model. Although its ferocious winds began to abate slowly, it took Mitch two days to drift southward to make landfall. Coastal regions and the offshore Honduran island of Guanaja were devastated. Mitch then began a slow westward drift through the mountainous interior of Honduras, finally reaching the border with Guatemala two days later on October 31.

Although the ferocity of the winds decreased during the westward drift, the storm produced enormous amounts of precipitation caused in part by the mountains of Central America. As Mitch's feeder bands swirled into its center from both the Caribbean and the Pacific Ocean to its south, the stage was set for a disaster of epic proportions. Taking into account the orographic effects by the volcanic peaks of Central America and Mitch's slow movement, rain fell at the rate of a foot or two per day in many of the mountainous regions. Total rainfall has been reported as high as 75 inches for the entire storm. The resulting floods and mud slides virtually destroyed the entire infrastructure of Honduras and devastated parts of Nicaragua, Guatemala, Belize, and El Salvador. Whole villages and their inhabitants were swept away in the torrents of flood waters and deep mud that came rushing down the mountainsides. Hundreds of thousands of homes were destroyed.

RE-BIRTH AND FLORIDA LAND FALL

The remnants of Mitch drifted northwestward as a weak depression and entered the Bay of Campreche on November 2. Over the warm waters and favorable conditions aloft, Mitch once more regained tropical storm status and began moving rapidly northeastward. It struck the western side of Mexico's Yucatan Peninsula which weakened it to tropical depression status once again. As Mitch moved back over the Gulf of Mexico, it regained tropical storm status for the third time. It raced northeastward and pounded Key West with tropical storm force winds and heavy rains on November 4-5. Some of the roofs and buildings damaged by Hurricane Georges in September fell victim to Mitch. Rains of six to eight inches were common in southern Florida and several tornadoes struck the region. At least 7 were injured when a tornado swept from Marathon to Key Largo. A second tornado touched down at Miramar north of Miami. At Fowey Rocks Lighthouse, just southeast of Miami, a wind gust of 73 mph was reported. Across south Florida, some 100,000 customers lost electrical power. One person was killed in the U.S. near Dry Tortugas when a fisherman died from a capsized boat. A second person was missing. Another person died as a result of an auto accident on a slick highway. Mitch passed through the Bahamas and finally became extratropical on November 5.

HONDURAS

Human toll: An estimated 6,500 dead with up to 11,000 still missing. Up to 1.5 million people displaced and homeless. Critical food, medicine, and water shortages. Hunger and near-starvation widespread in many villages. Epidemics feared as malaria, dengue, and cholera made appearance. Fever and respiratory illnesses widespread. Helicopters required to take supplies to areas cut off by floods, but were in short supply. Some survivors still reported clinging to roof tops, and isolated areas of Honduras had not received help as late as November 12. At least 20% of the country's population were homeless. Many of the unidentified dead were being buried in mass graves or their bodies were cremated. Tegucigalpa Mayor Cesar Castellanos, a likely candidate for Honduras' presidency in elections in 2001, and three others were killed when their helicopter crashed while surveying flood damage on Sunday,

November 1. On Wednesday, November 4, the U.S. Coast Guard called off its search for the schooner "Fantome" after debris and life jackets were found. Thirty-one members of the crew were presumed lost after the captain tried to shield the boat from Mitch by sailing south of Guanaja Island. The last contact from the ship was on October 27.

Structural damage: Infrastructure devastated. Whole villages washed away. Estimated 70-80 percent of transportation infrastructure destroyed. The majority of the country's bridges and secondary roads washed away. Even airports were under water. Helicopters were required for most rescues and aid because of transportation difficulties; communications disrupted. Fuel, electricity and running water scarce commodities. Damage so severe it may take 15 years to 20 years or more to rebuild. Some buildings 350 years old in capital city of Tegucigalpa were reported to be washed away completely. One third of all buildings in the capital were damaged by the floods. In outlying areas, over 25 small villages in the northern part of the country were swept away. Survivors were still clinging to roof tops a week or more after the storm. Heavy damage along coastline and off-shore islands from storm surge and hurricane-force winds. Severe damage inflicted on tourist resorts. Damage estimates of four billion dollars in Honduras alone.

Crop damage: At least 70 percent of crops destroyed, including 80 percent of the banana crop. Crop losses estimated at $900 million. Large warehouses and storage rooms for coffee flooded. Maize and corn crops devastated. The damage by Mitch to Honduran agricultural production will take years for recovery.

NICARAGUA

Human toll: An estimated 3800 dead with perhaps as many as 7,000 others still missing. Two million people directly affected and 500,000 - 800,000 homeless. Intense near-stationary rain bands over western Nicaragua on Thursday and Friday (October 29-30) caused tens of inches of rain to fall. The crater lake atop the dormant Casita volcano filled and part of the walls collapsed on Friday, October 30, causing mud flows that eventually covered an area ten miles long and five miles wide. At least four villages were totally buried in the mud that was several feet deep. Over 2,000 of the dead were from the areas around the collapsed volcano near Posoltega.

THE SAFFIR/SIMPSON HURRICANE SCALE

Hurricanes can be fickle storms with the observed or potential damage ranging from relatively minimal to catastrophic. The damage is dependent upon several factors. Not only is the intensity of the storm important, but geophyscial factors such as the size of the storm and its associated windfield, surrounding synoptic weather situation, coastal geological features, and the astronomical tide situation play an important part. The second major portion of the "equation for disaster" is the extent of economic, industrial, and residential development of the area affected.

Following numerous on-site investigations of hurricane damage, especially that from Hurricane Camille, Herbert Saffir devised a five-category damage scale in the early 1970's. The scale had the advantage of relating ranges of sustained winds to effects on vegetation and structures. Robert Simpson, a former director of the National Hurricane Center, added additional reference to expected storm surge (the rise of a body of water above astronomical tide due to a tropical cyclone).

In 1972, the Tropical Prediction Center (then known as the National Hurricane Center) adopted the Saffir/Simpson Hurricane Scale to relate hurricane intensity and damage potential. This scale uses the storm surge, central pressure, and/or the maximum sustained winds to classify Atlantic hurricanes into one of five categories.

WHAT IS A HURRICANE?

In August 1992, residents throughout southern Florida waited in fear of Andrew, the monstrous storm from the sea. His satellite picture looked terrifying, a compact, powerful swirl of clouds. Andrew had already killed four people in the Bahamas. As he approached Florida, thousands of people evacuated their homes in Miami, Miami Beach, and other communities that lay in the path of the huge storm. At the last minute, Andrew turned slightly south, sparing Miami, but with winds peaking at 164 mph (264 kph), the storm cut a swath of devastation through heavily populated towns in South Dade Country. Andrew moved west across Florida and regained strength over the Gulf of Mexico. He then turned north and bore down on southeastern Louisiana, where several more towns were severely damaged and more than 44,000 were left homeless.

In Florida, an incredible 63,000 homes were destroyed, and the Homestead Air Force Base was decimated. Thirty-three deaths were attributed to Andrew, as well as an astounding $30 billion in damage, making this the most expensive natural disaster to ever hit the United States.

WHERE HURRICANE GETS IT NAME

The word hurricane comes from the Spanish word huracan, meaning "great wind," or from similar words used by Caribbean Indian tribes to describe evil spirits, storm gods, and big winds.

Different parts of the world have different names for these massive storms. They are called cyclones in the Indian Ocean and near Australia, and typhoons in the western Pacific. In the rest of the Pacific Ocean, the Atlantic Ocean, the Caribbean, and the Gulf of Mexico they are called hurricanes. Similar storms in Australia are called willy-willies.

FAMOUS HURRICANES

Some hurricanes have become famous for the amount of death and damage they have caused. On September 8, 1900, a hurricane battered the island of Galveston, off the Texas coast. The city was devastated by high winds and a 15-foot (5 meter) surge of water that swept over the island. More than 6,000 people were killed. It was one of the worst natural disasters ever to hit the United States.

Another deadly hurricane hit Lake Okeechobee, Florida, in 1928. When the hurricane wind and waves broke an earthen dike, Lake Okeechobee emptied onto the flat farmland. In just a few hours, 1,836 people drowned and another 1,849 were injured.

Until Andrew in 1992, Hurricane Hugo was the United States' most expensive storm. During his violent visit he caused an estimated $7 billion in damage in the United States and another $3 billion in the Caribbean.

Death tolls from storms in the Western Hemisphere can't compare with those on the other side of the Earth. An estimated 300,000 lives were lost in 1881 when a typhoon hit the Haifong area of China. Some of the world's most disastrous storms occur along the densely populated areas of the Bay of Bengal. On October 7, 1737, a tropical cyclone hit Calcutta, India, killing more than 300,000 people. A similar storm in 1876 killed an estimated 100,000 people near the Bay of Bengal. When many of the dead were not promptly removed, several deadly diseases were spawned, eventually taking 100,000 more lives.

Death tolls have been even higher in modern times. The deadliest cyclone on record occurred in Bangladesh in 1970. Experts at the United Nations estimated the death toll to be greater than 500,000 from the storm itself and the diseases it caused. Another 100,000 residents of this tiny country were killed by a cyclone in 1991.

BIRTH PLACES OF HURRICANES

Most hurricanes form in two general bands 5° to 30° latitude north and south of the equator. Hurricanes cannot form closer to the equator than 5° because here the Coriolis force is too weak to provide the necessary spin to the storm.

Hurricanes also rarely form further than 30° north or south of the equator. Past that point, the stronger westerly winds in the upper levels of the atmosphere destroy developing hurricanes.

In the North Atlantic, hurricane season extends from June 1 to November 30, with most storms coming during August, September, and October. Storms in the Southern Hemisphere form during their summer and autumn seasons, November through June.

NAMING HURRICANES

Once a disturbance becomes a tropical storm, it is given a name. This gives meterologists an easy way to refer to it as they track the storm's progress.

Long ago, West Indian hurricanes were named after the particular saint's day on which they occurred. Later, hurricanes were identified by their latitude and longitude. This system was confusing, especially when more than one storm was in the area at one time.

In 1953 the U.S. Weather Bureau officially started naming hurricanes after women. The names were easy to pronounce, easy to remember, and were less likely to cause confusion than other methods. In the late 1970s men's names, as well as Hawaiian and Spanish names, were added. Now alphabetical lists alternating male and female names are used.

There are separate sets of names for hurricanes in the North Atlantic and for typhoons in the Pacific. The lists of names for North Atlantic hurricanes are repeated every six years. If a hurricane has been especially deadly or damaging, its name is removed from the list.

HURRICANE FACT SHEET

- A hurricane is a large whirling storm that normally measures 200 to 500 miles (320 to 800 km) across.
- On the average, six Atlantic hurricanes occur per year.
- A typical hurricane has sustained winds of 100-150 mph (160-240 kmph). Winds in some stronger storms may exceed 200 mph (320 kmph).
- The eye of a hurricane averages 14-25 miles (22-40 km) across. Large storms may have eyes up to 50 miles (80 km) across. The eye is relatively calm compared to the winds in the eye wall.
- The winds of a hurricane spin counterclockwise in the Northern Hemisphere and clockwise in the Southern Hemisphere.
- The hurricane season in the North Atlantic is June 1 to November 30. In the Southern Hemisphere the season is from November to June. Over the Western Pacific, the tropical cyclone season is never quite over.
- If the heat released by an average hurricane in one day could be converted to electricity, it could supply the United States' electrical needs for about six months.
- The heat energy released by a hurricane in one day can equal the energy released by the fusion of four hundred 20-megaton hydrogen bombs.
- As it travels across the ocean, a hurricane can pick up as much as two billion tons of water a day through evaporation and sea spray.
- Each second, some 2 million metric tons of air are circulated in, up, and out of the hurricane.

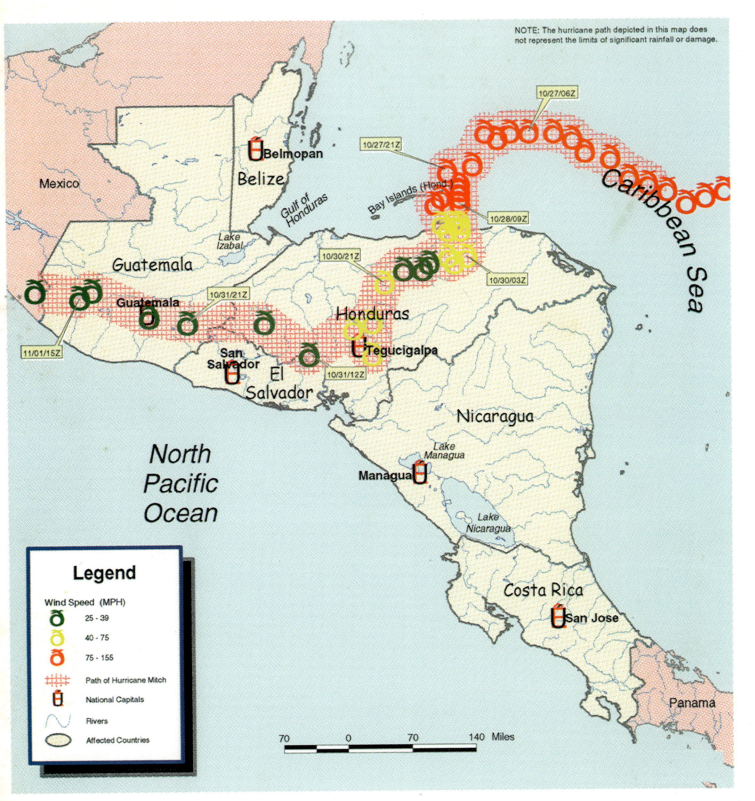

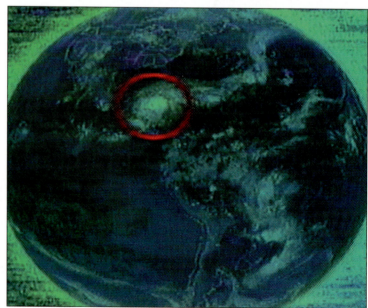

Daily Happenings

Printed with permission from *Honduras This Week*.
written by Jon Kohl

From a sofa in Massachusetts, my mother only saw telecast satellite images showing one massive gyrating hurricane. Its ghostly arms stretched from Mexico to South America completely blanketing Honduras. Worse, Hurricane Mitch's eye approached so closely to the North Coast of Honduras, where I worked, that in her mind it could have already blown my house -- and me -- to smithereens.

I should have anticipated when my call finally got through that – "I'm so glad you called! I had no idea what happened to you!" – she was nerve-racked and in tears. "All they keep mentioning on TV, every station, is La Ceiba, La Ceiba, La Ceiba."

"Well, actually, it's really not that bad, mom. There's been huge amounts of rain which have knocked out bridges and caused some flooding; the winds really aren't…"

"CNN has been showing pictures of flooded houses and people being evacuated," she interrupted. "They say 12 people are dead -- one American."

"How did CNN find that out?" I questioned indignantly. "We haven't even heard that. And who's taking those pictures anyway?" I was astounded that CNN knew so much when people in the middle knew so little. Then my mother repeated softly, "I'm so glad you called."

That was Wednesday, Oct. 28. At that time I still thought Mitch would stay out in the Caribbean and spare us. Unfortunately for Honduras, Class 5 Mitch, the most powerful category of hurricanes, suddenly turned 90 degrees straight for the mainland, marching through the middle of Honduras.

A car caught in the floodwaters.

OCTOBER 26, MONDAY

The rains had already started last night when I returned from a staff retreat in the United States. I had heard of a hurricane bound for Jamaica. But it was not until I found myself staring at the locked door of the laundromat with a bag of dirty laundry in my arms in pouring rain that Hurricane Mitch entered my life. I hardly had time to adjust. That evening the lights went out and I heard the surrounding houses release a collective yelp as their TVs blinked off. Fortunately for my roommate, Fito, and I, we were radio people.

Fito was a gaunt, light-skinned character with an overgrown goatee. Locals often asked if he were a "gringo" to which he fired back, "I am from Olanchito, 100 percent Honduran!" He learned English on the street, was president of the non-profit that managed Pico Bonito National Park south of La Ceiba, and loved radios. He pulled out his Sony nine-band short-wave radio and we listened to a report.

This is Radio San Isidro bringing the latest of Hurricane Mitch to the port city of La Ceiba. The Miami Hurricane Center forecasts torrential rains throughout the North Coast of Honduras. Take all precautions. If you live in low-lying areas start moving to higher ground. We're watching Mitch here on the Internet and, it is slowly heading north along the Mosquito Coast of eastern Honduras.

Fito scanned the FM bandwidth and found only three operating radio stations. "It looks like most stations stopped transmitting when the power went out. People have no television and little choice of radio stations," he observed.

Aside from radio stations we seemed to have sufficient bad weather supplies -- candles, batteries, flashlights, cooking gas, roof water collection buckets and granola.

OCTOBER 27, TUESDAY

The rain's incessant pounding of zinc roofs nearly deafened me trying to catch rainwater on the porch. Inside, the refrigerator was bleeding ice water all over the floor. Fito, a cleanliness nut, mopped it up before it had a chance to get out of hand. We had no running water, nonetheless, and despite his best efforts, mud on the floor, flies on partially washed dishes, and a toilet that did not flush all conspired to keep us busy.

The rains incessant pounding on zinc roofs was nearly deafening.

I imagined how much worse it would be to live without any sewage hook up or running water at all. People who lived on the city's margins hardly warranted its attention to build such utilities, but there was no where closer to the city a poor person could afford to build a house.

Mitch is now battering the Honduran island of Guanaja, 80 miles from La Ceiba and 35 miles from the mainland. It is moving west at only 6miles per hour. The heavy rains nevertheless are causing rivers to rise. The Cangrejal River has risen over 15 feet.

People climbed to higher ground hoping the water would not pursue them. But the rain kept coming.

Fortunately our house was solid, both legally and architecturally, and we lived on the second floor. Our property was well drained. Some saw it as a private shelter. For example, the married couple downstairs asked to borrow our gas stove since their electric one was enjoying a two-week storm vacation. Soon, enough greased up plantains and rice were cooking on our small stove to feed all 12 mouths.

Inspired, we went to the one remaining supermarket to stock up on non-perishables such as pasta, rice, beans, and potatoes. We threw in several boxes of corn flakes that, with rainwater and powdered milk, we thought would hold us tight.

The rain continued to fall without a care; I didn't care either as I knew we were safe.

OCTOBER 28, WEDNESDAY

Mitch is still slowly tracking west, parallel to the mainland, 60 miles from La Ceiba. Nonetheless last night several bridges were destroyed by the Cangrejal, Bonito, and other rivers.

These rivers, normally friendly neighbors of La Ceiba, had now cut it off. La Ceiba faced a roaring ocean to the north, treacherous rivers to the east and west, and impassable mountains of Pico Bonito to the south. Tonight 180,000 ceibenos would not only be in the dark, but trapped.

"We don't have this chance often, let's go see what's happening outside," Fito urged. The last time he could have driven into a hurricane was 24 years ago when Fifi dealt a devastating blow

Heavy rains are causing rivers to rise.

to Honduras. So we hopped in his truck and drove into the streets. It looked as if a glacier had passed through leaving water-filled pockmarks across the urban landscape. The rain rushed over streets, and people waded up to their waists in water. Low-lying houses flooded out. People and cars formed snaking gas and kerosene lines at the last two open gas stations.

We passed by the remains of the old Cangrejal bridge. Many river watchers bustled back and forth in the rain. Clearly though, the same question plagued everyone's mind as they studied a river on whose rocky bed tractors once descended to extract construction fill. The river had grown to 200 yards across stampeded by like 10,000 head of steer. Would the river stay in its bed or would it rise tonight to haunt La Ceiba?

After our tour we returned for an early lunch. Fito was heating some tortillas and twirls on the stove when he called, "Jon." He lifted the gas tank with one arm. At first his show of force impressed me, but he shook off my impression. "Jon, I estimate we have two meals worth of gas left. It was stupid not to check how much we had two days ago."

My head flushed. At first I wondered if we had yogurt, vegetables, and bread. But those foodstuffs had long since perished and if we couldn't cook the pasta and rice, our cabinet looked very poor. Without gas, I reasoned, we don't eat. Cornflakes and rainwater milk won't do. I felt my face tighten as I mumbled, "Fito, we got to find gas today."

We jumped once again into his car and joined hundreds of others searching for the same basic necessities; we drove to the gas company. Through pouring rain, we read a sign on the locked gate, "NO GAS." We visited a couple of sellers but everywhere gas was sold out last Monday. We were wasting our car gasoline as well, so we returned. The wife from downstairs came up again arms brimming with more plantains and rice. She dropped her head quietly as we turned her away. Now we had to think of ourselves.

Radio San Isidro reporting with the latest and perhaps gravest news. Hurricane Mitch has changed course and is heading for La Ceiba. This is no joke. Hurricane Mitch is coming to La Ceiba. We should note that Hurricane Fifi killed 10,000 Hondurans.

The remains of a bridge.

That was only class 2. The power of Mitch is catastrophic.

Before, the radio recounted other people's stories in Guanaja and the Mosquito Coast. Now it will be ours. I reminded myself that we had a tall, two-story house and neighbors all around. Even if the Cangrejal were to overflow its borders here, we were high up. And despite out low gas, we had collected over 15 gallons of rain water and had a high-tech Katadyn filter. We could trade water and pasta for gas!

Fito decided to make one more late trip to the the marine band radio from the office. He wanted to talk with friends and colleagues to coordinate whatever might need to be done.

I sat in candle light and reviewed. We had almost no gas. We lived three blocks from the Cangrejal which threatened to disgorge its contents. And we had a monster hurricane on the way.

I imagined it wasn't that bad. Consider other people's plight: the belly fat Cangrejal did overflow on the other side flooding poor communities, destroying houses and a *maquila* where several hundred young women once worked. Many families had been forced to abandon their houses and hide in shelters, not yet even knowing the hurricane was coming. Most had few supplies to begin with and lived in areas barely accessible to rescue units. I remembered what Fito had said about poor people's having to live in these places. The richer folk always have first choice.

Sure, we lived by the river, but a prescient architect built us on higher ground. We had mobile friends with food and resources. Soon we would have a marine band radio to keep us in contact. We had a truck, a multi-band radio, and a new can opener for some pineapples and tuna in the cabinet. Most people didn't enjoy all these things, and all else being equal under Mitch, we should be OK.

When Fito returned we ate and decided to cover up everything in our rooms, located windside of the house. I stood up my box spring against the window and secured it with three bungee cords. We moved mattresses, double-cassette radios, papers, plants, and anything else requiring protection to the safer living room.

As I laid on my mattress on the floor, Fito had

The power of Mitch is catastrophic. This picture shows a car washing down the river. It is almost standing-on-end at this time.

already gone to sleep. The room was remarkably tranquil. I peered through the open front door framing a background of darkness and driving rain. The silence of nothing except rain running off the roof tried to deceive me, make me think things were in order. Indeed, there was nothing to be seen through this portal, but I knew, I could almost hear the thousands of people outside, uncertain, frightened, waiting in the path of a class five hurricane.

OCTOBER 29, THURSDAY

Early in the morning Mitch made landfall, canons firing. It blasted restaurants and other tourist infrastructure along the beach. The storm ripped up trees and splintered modest houses, ripping the roofs off stronger ones. The Aguan River lost control and carried the entire village of Santa Rosa de Arguan out to sea, drowning dozens of people. Mitch even buzzed forest of the nearby national park off its own mountainside.

When I awoke at around 5 a.m., Fito was already listening to his Silvertronic 2-band radio with great AM reception. He said that Mitch was assaulting Trujillo, a historic town 60 miles west of La Ceiba. The storm had yet again capriciously backtracked to pound poor communities elsewhere. This I would read many days later in newspapers that were dedicating all their pages to the hurricane. So much information and not a single copy in La Ceiba. The storm had made sure to destroy not just trees and houses but communications: radio, TV, bridges, newspapers, even a neighborly chat over cold cokes proved impossible.

Hurricane Mitch was downgraded to class 1 and continued to move slowly over Trujillo. We had heard hopeful rumors that Mitch was heading back to sea, but regrettably it chose a path south into Honduras.

Ironically Columbus also landed in Trujillo on his fourth and final voyage in 1502. Legend has it that he chose the name "Honduras," which literally means "depths" in Spanish, after having come out of the depths of a great storm.

After Mitch passed, another great storm formed as hundreds of people surged toward any phone they could find – to call the radio station. They weren't trying to request a song or win prizes, they tried to discover if their brothers, grandparents, and mothers still lived.

The storm destroyed trees and houses and also communications by radio, TV and newspaper.

Filomena Prado calls in to tell her son in Trujillo that she is fine and would like him to call her.

Alicia Chavez says her parents are stuck on the other side of the Cangrejal in Barrio Pizati. She and her brother are okay and hope that Maria Antunez and Modesto Chavez come home soon. Since a branch fell on their phone line, they should call the neighbors.

Fito, known on the marine band as Amaras, called Colorado to learn his status. He was fine. So were Nutria, Blanco, Oso, and Salida. I considered calling my mom but I figured she never realized how close Mitch came to erasing La Ceiba from the map.

OCTOBER 30, FRIDAY

Ironically a week after the storm, I received an electronic Inter Press Service article stating that just as Mitch struck, a major report published by the United Nations, World Bank, U.S. government, and other major organizations declared that the state of Central America's environment is worsening thanks to ineffective and unenforced laws. The mudslides and flash floods, which earned most of Mitch's infamy, were as much human caused as natural.

Some politicians were starting to listen. Later I would read that the mayor of La Ceiba personally threatened to throw anyone in jail who extracted rocks outside the Cangrejal management plan. The Honduran Congress contemplated passing (and likely will) a law prohibiting people from living in dangerous locations that would then be converted into green areas.

At home we collected plenty of rainwater, a friend had given us another tank of gas, and nothing was damaged. Mitch wasn't so bad to us. The destruction did not have to happen and didn't to most well off like us. Nevertheless, had marginalized people been offered alternatives to living and deforesting steep slopes, had the foestry agency protected mountainsides from loggers who could buy them off, had construction companies extracted fill away from the bases of the Cangrejal bridges as per municipal law, had people been prohibited from living along rivers, most of this destruction would have been just fancy.

The mudslides and flashfloods which earned most of Mitch's infamy were as much human caused as natural.

The Most Deadly Hurricane to Strike the Western Hemisphere in 200 Years

Printed with permission from other sources.

In an awesome display of power and destruction, Hurricane Mitch will be remembered as the most deadly hurricane to strike the Western Hemisphere in the last two centuries! Not since the Great Hurricane of 1780, which killed approximately 22,000 people in the eastern Caribbean, was there a more deadly hurricane. Mitch struck Central America with such viciousness that it was nearly a week before the magnitude of the disaster began to reach the outside world. The death toll currently is reported as 11,000 with thousands of others missing. Though the final death toll will never be known, it is quite likely that Mitch directly killed more people than any Atlantic hurricane in over 200 years. More than three million people were either homeless or severely affected. In this extremely poor third world region of the globe, estimates of the total damage from the storm are at $5 billion and rising. The President of Honduras, Carlos Flores Facusse, claimed the storm destroyed 50 years of progress.

Assault on Central America

After threatening Jamaica and the Cayman Islands, Mitch moved westward and by 2100 UTC on October 27, the Category 5 storm was about 60 miles north of Trujilo on the north coast of Honduras. Preliminary wave height estimates north of Honduras during this time at the height of the hurricane are as high as 44 feet, according to one wave model. Although its ferocious winds began to abate slowly, it took Mitch two days to drift southward to make landfall. Coastal regions and the offshore Honduran island of Guanaja were devastated. Mitch then began a slow

Many buildings were damaged by Hurricane Mitch.

westward drift through the mountainous interior of Honduras, finally reaching the border with Guatemala two days later on October 31.

Although the ferocity of the winds decreased during the westward drift, the storm produced enormous amounts of precipitation caused in part by the mountains of Central America. As Mitch's feeder bands swirled into its center from both the Caribbean and the Pacific Ocean to its south, the stage was set for a disaster of epic proportions. Taking into account the orographic effects by the volcanic peaks of Central America and Mitch's slow movement, rain fell at the rate of a foot or two per day in many of the mountainous regions. Total rainfall has been reported as high as 75 inches for the entire storm. The resulting floods and mudslides virtually destroyed the entire infrastructure of Honduras and devastated parts of Nicaragua, Guatemala, Belize, and El Salvador. Whole villages and their inhabitants were swept away in the torrents of flood waters and deep mud that came rushing down the mountainsides. Hundreds of thousands of homes were destroyed.

Re-birth and Florida Landfall

The remnants of Mitch drifted northwestward as a weak depression and entered the Bay of Campeche on November 2. Over the warm waters and favorable conditions aloft, Mitch once more regained tropical storm status and began moving rapidly northeastward. It struck the western side of Mexico's Yucatan Peninsula which weakened it to tropical depression status once again. As Mitch moved back over the Gulf of Mexico, it regained tropical storm status for the third time. It raced northeastward and pounded Key West with tropical storm force winds and heavy rains on November 4-5. Some of the roofs and buildings damaged by Hurricane Georges in September fell victim to Mitch. Rains of six to eight inches were common in southern Florida and several tornadoes struck the region. At least seven were injured when a tornado swept from Marathon to Key Largo. A second tornado touched down at Miramar north of Miami. At Fowey Rocks Lighthouse, just southeast of Miami, a wind gust of 73 mph was reported. Across south Florida,

Total rainfall has been reported as high as 75 inches for the entire storm in some places, some of the streets could not hold all the water.

some 100,000 customers lost electrical power. One person was killed in the U.S. near Dry Tortugas when a fisherman died from a capsized boat.

Within four days of its birth as a tropical depression on October 22, Mitch had grown into a Category 5 storm on the Saffir-Simpson Hurricane Scale. By 2100 UTC on October 26, the monster storm had deepened to a pressure of 905 millibars with sustained winds of 155 knots (180 mph) and gusts well over 200 mph! Mitch thus became tied for the fourth strongest Atlantic hurricane on record based upon barometric pressure values. Though the pressure began rising six hours later, Mitch remained at Category 5 status for a continuous period of 33 hours - the longest continuous period for a Category 5 storm since the 36 consecutive hours by Hurricane David in 1979. In addition, Mitch maintained sustained winds of 155 knots for 15 hours - the third longest period of such winds on record after the continuous 18 hours of 155 knot winds or higher by Hurricane Camille in 1969 and Hurricane Dog in 1950. Though exact comparisons are suspect due to differing frequencies in observation times (3-hourly versus 6-hourly observations) and a bias in earlier years toward higher estimated wind speeds, it is quite apparent that Mitch was one of the stronger storms ever recorded in the Atlantic.

Infrastructure devastated. Whole villages washed away. Estimated 70 - 80 percent of transportation infrastructure destroyed. The majority of the country's bridges and secondary roads washed away. Even airports were under water. Helicopters were required for most rescues and aid because of transportation difficulties; communications disrupted. Fuel, electricity and running water scarce commodities. Damage so severe it may take 15 years to 20 years or more to rebuild. Some buildings 350 years old in capital city of Tegucigalpa were reported to be washed away completely. One third of all buildings in the capital were damaged by the floods. In outlying areas, over 25 small villages in the northern part of the country were swept away. Survivors were still clinging to roof tops a week or more after the storm. Heavy damage along coastline and off-shore islands from storm surge and hurricane-force winds. Severe damage inflicted on tourist

Note the school bus standing in about ten feet of water.

resorts. Damage estimates of four billion dollars in Honduras alone.

Tropical Storm Mitch Uprooted Crops

For five days, more than 400 people in this isolated company town deep in the heart of banana country huddled in the rafters of their wooden homes and a dilapidated school without food or sleep. Rain pounded down relentlessly, and flood waters rose to within inches of the beams, threatening to topple the shaky buildings and sweep them away.

Avilio Rodas, 52, could feel his frail home twist and sway beneath him in the strong current. He and 23 others spent days and night stepping gingerly from one third-floor beam to another, trying to keep the building balanced and upright in 20 feet of rushing water.

"We felt lost, like we had no chance," said Rodas. "We were just waiting for the house to fall over and become part of the river."

Against all odds, Tropical Storm Mitch did not claim any lives among the 1,200 workers and residents of La Ceibita, a plantation town that is owned and managed by one of the largest private employers in Honduras.

Throughout the country flooding and landslides caused lots of problems.

But the sense of relief felt by survivors such as Rosa, who has worked for Chiquita since he was 9, has largely been supplanted by worry about the future. Banana industry and government officials said that flooding destroyed not just the banana crop, but the plants themselves–in other words, virtually the entire banana industry in Honduras. The damage has already thrown thousands of people out of work and is expected to wipe out $255 million in annual banana exports over the next two years before the industry might begin to recover.

"This is by far the most devastating loss the industry has encountered in the last 25 years," said Steven Warshaw, Chiquita's president and chief operating officer. "We think all or close to all of our production of bananas is destroyed."

The banana industry blossomed in the early 1900's and was once so important to Honduras the term "Banana Republic" was coined to describe its influence here. Absent is a powerful government with the resources to develop the country, banana barons built many of the country's roads, rail lines, ports and electricity

Rain pounded down relentlessly for days and floodwaters rose some places 20 to 40 feet. As you can see in this picture cars were piled on top of each other.

plants and wielded enormous political influence.

Chiquita officials in Honduras, which is the world's fourth-largest banana producer and exports about 6 billion bananas a year, said the company lost nearly 11 million plants on its 17,300 acres. Countrywide, government officials said, about 90 percent of the industry was destroyed, or more than 27 million plants.

The destruction was not confined to bananas, or to Honduras. Agriculture across Central America, where large portions of the impoverished populations rely on farming which was devastated by Mitch, which drowned crops with up to six feet of rain.

More than 14 million pounds of coffee beans were ruined in Costa Rica, and Guatemala lost perhaps a quarter of its coffee harvest, officials there said. Thousands of acres of sugar cane were destroyed. Tobacco plants in Costa Rica, Honduras and Nicaragua, which exports some of the world's finest cigars were severely damaged. Pineapples, cantaloupes, honeydew melons and, other fruits and vegetables were ravaged.

Because agriculture plays such an important role in the economies of Central America, where per capita incomes average about $1,900 per year, crop losses translate directly into job losses. In Honduras, for example, about 54 percent of the work force is employed by the agricultural sector.

"Try to imagine it; we lost everything," said Chiquita worker Lionel Rivera while sweeping an ankle-deep layer of soupy mud from his home in the small community of Omita. Outside, the street was littered with mattresses, furniture and electrical appliances, all covered with a foot of muck.

"We're great because we're alive," said his neighbor, retired Chiquita worker Juan Sabilloin, whose daughter in Miami sent money for a new mattress. "Everything else is horrible."

The road between the banana centers of La Lima and El Progreso is lined with shacks hastily constructed from torn-down billboards and makeshift tents assembled from plastic sheets, tattered curtains and whatever else could be salvaged from the mud.

Carlos Humberto Turcious, a machine operator for a small agricultural company, said that in less than an hour, flood water in his hometown of La Democracia rose to his chest,

Piles of debris left after floodwaters receded.

washing away 45 houses, including his. Now, he and 18 relatives and friends were sleeping in a 12- by 12-foot shack on the median strip of a highway. "There's going to come a time when someone says, 'Move' and where are we going to go?" he asked.

The dirt road to La Ceibita, about an hour's drive east of San Pedro Sula, the industrial capital of Honduras, is lined with mangled, wilting banana plants, each 10 to 12 feet high. The plants were submerged in flood waters for at least 72 hours, which drowned them, industry officials said.

Rufino Alvarez Garcia, 42, who has worked for Chiquita for 29 years and has lived through other floods at La Ceibita, said the water rose 20 feet in about six hours blocking the retreat of about 400 residents to higher ground. Before the storm, he said, he built a raft from banana plants as a precaution and then spent the first few hours of the deluge rescuing neighbors and ferrying them to the school. The current got too strong.

"For the next five days, 115 people balanced, themselves on the school's rafters, about eight inches above 20-foot-deep flood waters swirling below. They relieved themselves through a window. They couldn't sleep. There was no food. Some of the men tried to swim for help, but the current was too powerful and pushed them back. A few managed to swim to the tops of nearby coconut trees, Alvarez said, "to grab fruit so the children would have something to drink.

"I was scared," he said. "I've been through floods, but I'd never seen anything like this."

Finally, as the waters started to recede, a group of men swam with bicycles slung over their shoulders to an elevated rail line, then pedaled, walked and swam to a town about eight miles away, where they collected food and water for their families clinging to the rafters.

Today, townspeople were shoveling mud from their homes and fretting about their future. Chiquita has temporarily laid off almost all its 7,400 banana workers in Honduras while it maps out a reconstruction plan. It has promised to keep its community schools open to continue providing workers and their families with medical insurance, housing and utility service, and to provide employees with financial assistance that will get most through the end of January. After that,

One hundred and fifteen people who were stranded in a school balanced themselves on the rafters for five days without food or sleep.

workers will be eligible for interest-free loans. In the meantime, they are allowed to salvage any bananas they can, either to eat or sell at the local market.

Chiquita officials said they will pay to plow company land and buy seeds for employees who want to form cooperatives and farm the plantations until they can be replanted with bananas. They said they are working on a master plan of phased replanting that could take years to complete.

Meanwhile, residents of La Ceibita say they hope the new spirit of brotherhood developed over the past few weeks will see them through.

"We've left our differences behind; if one can get food, it's food for everybody," said Alvarez. "Life is very different. There's no work. We have no electricity. We have no water. But at least we have our lives."

For towns like the once thriving community of Posoltega, nestled on rich soil beneath the Casitas Volcano in Nicaragua's mountainous northwest, Mitch was the apocalypse. Close to noon on Oct. 30, after the hurricane had dumped three days of rain into Castita's crater, the mountainside burst with what villages described as the angry roar of a jetliner. It hurled mud, water and rock onto Tosoltega's rooftops," a terrible, towering wall that just fell out of the clouds," says Santo Diaz, 25. Diaz gathered his elderly father, mother, sister and two brothers to escape–but the avalanche claimed them. He was still clutching their hands as they were buried alive.

In Honduras, Mitch spawned the worst floods in 200 years. As Vice President William Handel helicoptered over the deluged Ulua River valley, he saw three people trapped on a patch of high ground, waving frantically. The waters rose so fast that the chopper couldn't land–and Handel, just yards away, watched them drown, tossed like rag dolls in the current.

As the gravity of the disaster reached around the world, close to $100 million in aid poured in.

Many if not most of Mitch's victims were youngsters–including not only those who drowned but also those whose malnourished bodies were no match for the deadly septic infections set free in the waters. Says Charles Compton, local head of Plan International relief

Water gushes out of these windows.

organization. "We have to keep starvation and infection from claiming as many victims as the hurricane did." When the final tally is in, the assertions of a staggering toll may well be borne out. Those whom the floodwaters did not kill face the problems of isolation, starvation, disease and neglect–the normal stuff of tragedy in Central America, made hundreds of times worse by Mitch's murderous rains.

In Nicaragua alone, much of the landscape looks as barren as the moon. Starving, sallow-skinned children, many suffering cholera from the fetid waters that destroyed their homes, begged for food on the crumbled, mud-slick roads between Managua and the flooded northern sierras.

When the president of Honduras, Carlos Flores was stranded by flood waters during an inspection trip on October 31, two U.S. military Black Hawk helicopters plucked him from a hilltop and ferried him to safety. But the military hastens to point out that American troops were able to ride instantly to the rescue only because they have a constant presence in Honduras.

MANAGUA, NICARAGUA–This part of the world has seen more than its share of pain and suffering. So it seems especially cruel when natural calamity suddenly compounds the age-old problems of poverty, war, and impotent government. But that's precisely what happened when Hurricane Mitch roared up out of the Caribbean basin and barreled into Honduras' economic heartland, pummeling it during a five-day march across Central America.

Rafael Hernandez lost two siblings in the mudslide and had to walk 20 miles to get to two other relatives who were hospitalized. Encountered on the side of a mud-filled highway, Hernandez had big bags of rice and beans strapped to his back, sustenance for the injured in the hospital. "The people have nothing to eat," he said.

According to the IFRC, volunteers have trudged through mud and flooded areas on foot to deliver supplies because their trucks continue to bog down in mud. One Red Cross team in El Salvador formed a human chain across a flooded river to pass along food and clothes to victims because the bridges were swept away by raging waters.

These people are trying to get some of their belongings out of their flooded home.

"One of the biggest problems throughout the region, especially in Honduras, is the lack of drinking water," said Auilar. Water is unsafe to drink because sewage and thousands of corpses have been floating in swirling, swollen rivers. Drinking contaminated water could pass along deadly water-borne diseases such as cholera and dengue fever, and cases of diarrhea already have turned up in some shelters.

Mexico has been a particularly helpful neighbor, launching one of the biggest airlifts in history to Honduras and Nicaragua. In addition, Great Britain sent two Royal Navy ships to help with search-and-rescue operations and transport storm victims to safety, and French mining experts were en route to Nicaragua to help remove landmines unearthed by floodwaters.

Two boys swimming in the street.

Helicopters were used to rescue many people.

Someone's graduation cap lies beside the grave with a wooden stick cross.

The beginning of the creek bed.

Hurricane Mitch
Disaster to the Nth Degree

Reprinted with permission by *Nica News*.

October, the month of the year when more rain falls than in any other month, was particularly vicious this year. Rains had been falling regularly throughout the country, skies were generally cloudy and grey, and people were thinking that the country was nearing the end of one of the best rainy seasons in the last 12 years.

Due to the El Nino climactic phenomenon, rainfall had been irregular and Nicaragua was plagued with droughts of varying degrees, generally having a negative impact on farm production.

This year, after a good first crop had been pulled in, farmers and government agriculture officials were expecting an excellent second crop and beginning to make plans for the third planting of beans, scheduled for late November and early December.

Rain was heavy and some people even attributed the strong tremors centered in the town of Ticuantepe, 18 kilometers south of Managua, to an overabundance of rain. Those earth movements put a scare into many residents in Ticuantepe and surrounding areas.

Damage was slight for the most part, but people were shaken and wary of the potential of Nature's wrath.

On Wednesday, October 21, reports of a hurricane approaching the Caribbean seaboard were issued by the Nicaraguan Institute for Territorial Studies (Ineter).

The hurricane, named Mitch, was heading straight for the coast, bringing back fearful memories of the last hurricane to strike Nicaragua: Joan in October 1988. Later that night, the capital Managua was witness to one of the most spectacular lightning storms and torrential downpours of the year.

Rain was heavy and some people attributed the heavy tremors centered in the town of Ticuantepe to an overabundance of rain.

Mitch then headed straight for the coast, bringing back fearful memories of the last Hurricane, Joan, which struck in October 1988.

Hurricane Mitch had an awesome display of power and destruction with 72 inches of rain recorded in some places.

The same happened in the late afternoon the next day. Data received from meteorological stations indicated that some 100 mm. (almost 4 inches) had fallen in less than an hour. The main arteries of the capital were flooded for a brief time, other roads were damaged partially, but everything was back to normal in short order, save for a few more potholes.

Monitoring Mitch

On Friday, October 23, the hurricane watchers reported that Mitch had veered north and was about to sweep the Caribbean coastline of neighboring Honduras. A collective sigh of relief was heard. However, given past experience with tropical storms that suddenly change course or that spin off cloud formations laden with precipitation, people throughout the country remained wary.

Rain continued to drizzle down all over the country on Saturday and another lesser tremor in Ticuantepe focused people's attention on the ever-present possibility of a major quake. The rains continued in the coming days and reports began to come in from the Bay Islands of Honduras which had been virtually scoured by the unprecedented 285 km. an hour winds of Hurricane Mitch.

The torment was very slow moving compared to most hurricanes, but at least it was moving and expectations were that it would continue to do so.

Then, Mitch stopped and remained stationary off the north coast of Honduras, an unheard of phenomenon, while its winds maintained their destructive force.

Satellite images of Central America showed a swirling mass of heavy cloud blanketing the entire region. The rain continued without let up and became more intense.

By the middle of the last week of October, the first reports of flooding were being received. The waters of Lake Managua were rising, inundating poor neighborhoods and squatter settlements along its shoreline near the capital.

Rivers in the northwest and north central regions were rising rapidly. Then it broke loose in the form of the worst natural disaster in the history of the country in terms of the area affected.

Floodwaters cover the main road.

Disaster? Emergency? It's Bad!

Bridges were being washed away, people in low-lying areas were climbing trees to get out of the rising flood, entire cities were cut off, and numerous reports of deaths of people being swept away in torrents were coming in.

To give an idea of how much rain was falling, the weather station near the city of Chinandega in northwest Nicaragua had over a meter of rain (about 40 inches) in over three days, with almost half a meter falling on Friday, October 30th.

Civil Defense, which is under the control of the Army, was hard pressed to respond to all the calls for help coming in via radio, telephone, or transmitted verbally by those who had managed to get out of affected areas.

Helicopters are the ideal vehicle for reaching areas cut off by flooding, but the incessant rain, inclement weather, and a permanent eerie mist hanging over the country limited visibility to less than a kilometer.

Before the arrival of helicopters from Mexican, Panama, and the United States, there were less than 10 helicopters available in the country and the air force had limited funds for fuel purchases. Texaco stepped in providing fuel for the flights, but more helicopters were needed.

Plea for International Aid

The government reacted immediately to the reports of death and destruction and put out an urgent plea for international assistance, arranging meetings with major donors to the country.

The Sandinista opposition party called on the government to declare a State of Emergency but President Aleman was reluctant to do so. He reasoned that such a declaration would put a brake on the economic recovery process underway in the country.

He also cited the concern that farmers could then use such a declaration to justify not repaying loans they had out from the banks– a common enough practice in Nicaragua in the past– and said this would discourage foreign investment.

Another concern he raised was that non-governmental organizations, or NGOs, many run by people unsympathetic to the present administration's policies, would be freed up to organize.

With $950 million more that U.S. Congress has approved, it will make a total of $1,200 million that will help 17 million people protect themselves from contagious diseases. Seven hundred health clinics will be built and put into operation.

Mitch Batters North Coast

Printed with permission from *Honduras This Week*

OCTOBER 30, 1998

Tens of Thousands Left Homeless in Wake of Hurricane's Destruction

TEGUCIGALPA–The greatest damage has occurred along the Atlantic coast in the departments of the Bay Islands, Cortes, Atlantida, Colon, Yoro and Gracias a Dios.

The area most affected has been the island of Guanaja, where more than 80 percent of the buildings have reportedly been destroyed while the roofs of shelters holding more than a thousand persons were blown off by strong winds.

In Roatan, the largest of the Bay islands, electricity is out, airports are flooded and there has been enormous environmental damage.

Photo at right: Man mourning friends and relatives.

This village was inundated with sand and mud plus the water. There was from three to seven inches of sand and mud in the street and the houses. David Stutzman calculated 6,000 cubic yards of sand just in these streets. (Not including houses, yards, etc.) These ladies were digging a path to reach the street level from their homes.

Mitch Sweeps Away Children's Entire World

Printed with permission from *USA Today*

NOVEMBER 5, 1998

Hospitals and shelters in Nicaragua are filled with orphans, many of whose parents died while trying desperately to insure their safety.

CHINANDEGA, NICARAGUA–Five-year-old Isetta Velasquez lies injured and alone in her hospital bed, crying for her father and mother.

Her right shoulder fractured, her left arm in a splint, her face covered with cuts, Isetta has no idea what happened to her. Or why her parents don't come when she calls.

"We think both her parents died in the floods," says Lorena Janis, a nurse at the Mauricio Abdulah Hospital in Chinandega. "She just cries most of the day. The only reason we even know her name is that a distant relative came in the first day she was here, but she hasn't been back since."

The children of Nicaragua have borne the brunt of Hurricane Mitch, one of the most violent Atlantic storms on record. In a horrific twist of fate, many of them have been left orphaned by the actions of desperate parents trying only to save their children's lives.

Officials say children are the most numerous among the survivors in Nicaragua.

Authorities say many parents helped their children up trees before being sucked away by raging landslides. Or the children scampered up trees or onto the roofs of their houses on their own, seeking shelter from the cascading walls of water and mud.

Whatever the case, officials estimate that hundreds of children have been left orphaned by Mitch.

Mitch's rains battered Nicaragua for days, flooding out residents near Lake Managua and

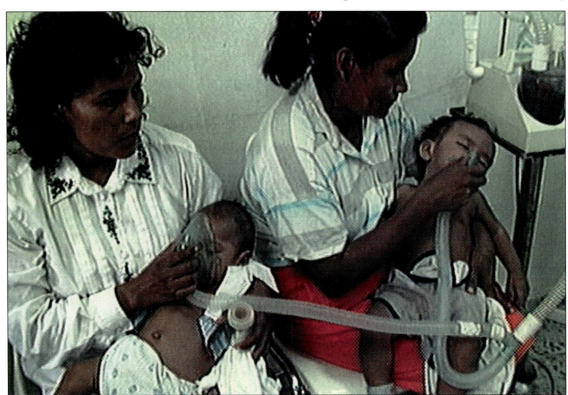

Hospitals and shelters are filled with orphans, many of whose parents died while trying desperately to ensure their safety.

causing devastating landslides near the Honduran border.

"There are so many kids on their own now," says Sister Socorro Castillo, a nurse and nun working at Chinandega's other hospital, the Espana, where children lie two to a bed.

When one side of the volcano collapsed, it sent earth, rock and mud hurtling into the village of Posoltega far below. As deadly debris slammed into the home of 13-year-old Anielka Majorga, she and a neighbor scrambled up a tree, then dashed to a field of sugar cane on higher ground. For four days, they waited in the torrential rain without food or shelter until rescuers found them.

"My brother and sister, my parents, the river took them all away," she said from her hospital bed. Anielka spoke without emotion, her eyes gazing into the distance.

Asked if Anielka was heavily medicated for her pain, nurse Castillo answered: "No, all the kids are like this. They all have the same horrible look on their faces, that empty stare, the sad eyes that tell you something very bad has happened."

Four-year-old Zelena Bargas doesn't know yet that her parents and three siblings are dead. Her uncle Orlando Reyes, who lives in Chinadega, can't bring himself to tell her yet. For the moment, he's told her only that they are ill.

"When I got here to the hospital, she was sleeping, having a nightmare," Reyes said. "She was screaming, 'The water is taking me'."

Reyes says he'll take care of the little girl with the sad brown eyes. Covered with cuts, she lies in her hospital bed under a bloodstained pink blanket. Her right leg is in a cast and an intravenous drip is in her arm. She idly plays with a stuffed animal.

"I've lost my father, mother, brother and sister," Reyes says. "Everyone is gone because of this flood. She's all that's left of my family."

A few miles down the road from Chinandega, corpses protrude from the mud. Lifeless hands reaching toward the sky as if calling for help.

"There are still many, many bodies in there," Adria Arias, a health ministry worker, said, pointing to a sugar cane field. Arias said the water swept its victims off the mountain, carrying them miles to their resting place in a plantation.

Officials estimate that hundreds of children have been left orphaned.

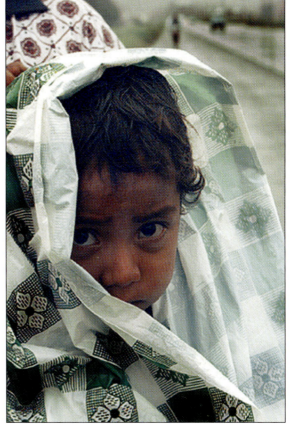

In remote areas, workers sprayed gasoline on corpses from helicopters.

The lucky ones- thousands driven from their homes but still alive- were ferried by helicopter to shelters in and around Chinandega. Pilots spotted hundreds more walking in the desolate terrain toward larger towns. But some 300 people refuse to leave their homes on the volcano's slopes.

"We're bringing food and medicine for them," Guadamuz said. "But we have very little food here." He warned of a "very dangerous medical situation."

About 700 people were crowded into a school in the town of Chichigalpa.

"Some of these people were brought in by helicopter, many of them walked miles to get here," said Maria Teresa Ordonez, a volunteer at the shelter. "They made human chains to cross the rivers."

At the shelter, dozens sleep on the tile floors in the converted classrooms. "We have no idea where these people will go," Ordonez said, "Or when we can open the school again."

Eventually, most will make it home again. But many won't have the chance to mourn their dead because their loved ones were dumped into a common grave in an effort to stave off epidemics.

Wednesday afternoon, almost the entire village of San Pablo di Posoltega turned out for the only proper burial the area has seen among the hundreds killed by Mitch.

Eleven-year-old Isias Santali, who was struck in the back by a tree limb, bled to death during surgery Tuesday at the hospital.

The family had no money for a coffin, so the hospital gave them a simple wooden one. It was carried to the cemetery atop a tractor.

Weeping villagers walked behind the vehicle to the graveyard with blue wooden crosses.

"This is the only funeral we can have," said the boy's grandfather Sergio Santali, who lost his daughter, Isias' mother, her husband and the couple's three other children in the disaster.

"Thank God we could at least bury him," he said. "Because none of the others got a decent burial."

Entire villages were washed away. Thousands were missing...

Mitch's Toll May Hit 7,000

Printed with permission from *USA Today*.

NOVEMBER 3, 1998

As rescuers dug through tons of mud, debris and decomposing bodies Monday, officials of flood-ravaged Honduras and Nicaragua said the death toll from Hurricane Mitch could climb as high as 7,000.

"Honduras is mortally wounded. There are corpses everywhere," Honduran President Carlos Flores Facusse said. "The most conservative calculations of the dead are in the thousands, not hundreds."

If the death toll is confirmed it would make Mitch the second-deadliest storm ever in Central America after Hurricane Fifi, which killed an estimated 10,000 people in 1974.

"Entire villages have been destroyed," said Timothy Hensall, a Toronto native volunteering at the Red Cross in Managua, Nicaragua. "People are starving to death. People are freezing to death."

Mitch has almost entirely dissipated, but its remnants could cause increased rain in south Florida by Wednesday or Thursday.

Though Honduras and Nicaragua were hit hardest by Mitch, nearly 150 additional deaths have been reported in El Salvador and Guatemala, Costa Rica and Panama also have reported casualties.

Officials also said Monday that 10 Americans and a Guatemalan were killed when a plane operated by the Texas-based Living Water Teaching Mission crashed Sunday in rains in Guatemala.

Also Monday, Coast Guard crews found debris from a sailing ship that vanished off Honduras last week with 31 crew members on board while trying to evade Mitch. Rescuers were hopeful that crew members of the Fantome, a 71-year-old schooner that is the flagship of the Windjammer Barefoot Cruises' tall ships, were still alive on the ship's life rafts.

Honduras is mortally wounded. There are corpses everywhere.

This scene was taken to the right of the bridge. The parts of foundations seen in the foreground are all that remain of the homes once located along the river's edge. The bridge in the background was so badly damaged that it is closed until it can be repaired.

Comayaguela, shown here, experienced mass destruction. Accented by the heat, the smell of rotting refuse and bodies was often overwhelmingly strong. It was all we could do to keep from vomiting. Walking was our only means of transportation so there was no escaping the reality of devastation that was experienced in this city.

Nicaragua Digs Out of Mud Fights Stench of Death

Printed with permission from *USA Today* and *Nica News*.

NOVEMBER 4, 1998

Mitch-spawned mudslides, floods sending death toll estimates near 7,000 as survivors search villages, try to stem tide of infection, disease.

CHICHIGALPA, NICARAGUA–First there was a roar, then a monstrous wave of mud on the horizon. In an instant, entire towns were swallowed up.

"The wave was coming up in the air; it looked like a line of helicopters" flying in low over the foliage of El Ojochal, Miguel Angel Ortiz said from a shelter.

It was what villagers feared most: After days of pounding rain, the craterlake high above them on the Casitas volcano in northwest Nicaragua had overflowed. The two rivers that drain the lake had joined to form one big deluge.

The 30-square mile avalanche of mud buried and killed up to 1,500 people, Vice President Enrique Bolanos said. Several villages near the volcano were also destroyed.

"We perhaps will never know how many people died," Bolanos said.

If the death toll is confirmed it would make Mitch the second-deadliest storm in Central America after Hurricane Fifi, which killed an estimated 10,000 in 1974.

Late Monday, another small mudslide on the northern slope of the volcano wiped out 34 houses, but there were no apparent casualties.

Now, rescuers are turning their attention from burying the dead to finding and rescuing the survivors, like Ortiz.

For three days, he and his family were trapped on the hilltop near the volcano without food or drinking water, under a driving rain

The mountain known as Casita HIll, which collapsed, causing a huge mudslide, which engulfed the whole village in a river of mud, rocks and trees and killing an estimated 2,500 people.

brought on by Hurricane Mitch. The mud that covered El Ojochal and seven nearby villages in a miles-wide swath was too unstable to walk over safely.

Other El Ojochal survivors, 45 in all, struggled to the hilltop, now an island in a sea of mud. The healthy men among them made brief, desperate forays onto the shimmering mud to look for survivors and rescue the injured. Nine people were found.

"The injured people stank because their wounds were infected, and the dead stank even worse," Ortiz said.

They walked out Monday, because the ground had firmed somewhat and "because we would have died there if we had not," Ortiz said.

The first helicopters that reached the region found decomposing bodies everywhere, some with just limbs sticking out of the mud.

At first, soldiers struggled to bury the bodies where they lay. But with fear of epidemics growing, volunteers set out to burn the bodies.

"We need the government to send us gasoline if they want to avoid an epidemic," said Robert Lopez Marcia of Chichigalpa's emergency commission.

At an improvised shelter in a Chichigalpa elementary school, doctors stitched wounds and performed other minor surgery on people evacuated from the mountains. The doctors were in desperate need of medicine, antibiotics and bandages, and there was little clean water or food. Children lay on desks with bloody bandages on their heads.

All along the Pan American highway, thousands of people walked in the pouring rain Tuesday, some leaving the disaster area, others going in to search for family members.

Few got very far. Dozens of bridges were washed out and roads were damaged. Bystanders pitched in to help cars and ox carts stuck in the mud.

Among them were dozens of children who ran up and down the villages screaming "Mama" and crying. They had become separated from their parents during the mudslides. Several feared their parents were buried beneath the mud.

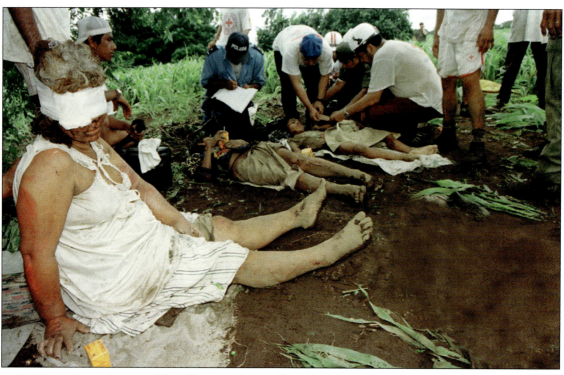

Other El Ojochal survivors, 45 in all, struggled to the hilltop now an island in a sea of mud. The healthy men among them made brief, desperate forays onto the shimmering mud to look for survivors and rescue the injured. Nine people were found alive.

Eric Rio, 26, and his wife, Ruth Reyes, 25, hiked for hours through deep mud into Barrio Chamorro to check on family and friends. They found none.

"We saw about 10 bodies, all very decomposed," Rio said.

Nearby, they passed another resident, Richardo Vaca, who was trying to uncover a corpse that had only its hand sticking out from the mud. After two hours of trying , he stopped digging and began crying.

"Everywhere you look is death," Vaca said. "Nothing but death."

On Sunday, November 8 we went to Posoltega, where a volcanic mudslide had killed an estimated 2500 people. Late Friday, October 30, residents heard what some described as the sound of many airplanes. One survivor told us he heard an explosion and then, minutes later, being engulfed in a river of mud, rocks and trees.

The area is in the rural zone of the municipality of Posoltega. Seven villages were affected: El Porvenir, Velsaya, Ojochal, Maria del Pilar, Villa Sandino, Tolotar, and Torrion.

We found local guides who had lived in El Porvenir to take us up the slope. We drove as far as we could and then walked the last three miles to the top of the volcano's skirt where the village of El Porvenir used to be.

As we walked through beautiful countryside, the only reminders that something was amiss were the discarded latex gloves on the ground. Then we came across the body of a dead cow, marking the beginning of destruction. The rolling hills and verdant green fields we had crossed changed abruptly to a vast expanse of rock and gravel stretching for 400 meters and flowing for miles downhill.

My diaphragm was convulsing and my eyes watering, as I tried to keep from vomiting. The smell of the cow was all but overpowering.

"These were once rolling hills and sugar cane fields," our local guide told us. "Over there used to be the health center," he said, pointing at a large rock.

We passed a plastic basket filled with clothes on the side of the path. It was so odd to see anything of value lying about unattended in

Distributing food and clothing to all the homeless people.

Nicaragua.

We saw our first corpse a few minutes later. He was a large male, laying on his back on top of the mud, arms outstretched as if in supplication. We saw more than 25 corpses in the next few hours.

We had arrived before the health service workers had reached the top. We could see the smoke from the bodies they were burning downslope. The plumes of smoke got closer as the body burners made their way toward us, carrying out their grisly work.

It was after we talked with them that we understood the aplomb with which they soaked the corpses in gasoline and then torched them. With so many dead, the danger of disease outweighed the natural desire to give the victims a proper burial. They had been burning bodies for eight days.

On the way back we passed the same cow that had given me so much trouble on the way in. The stench of death was all around me, but I was fine. I was amongst the living and going home.

One of the leaders of the health service crew read me the statistics, comparing the number of survivors with the last census. The figures were staggering:

	Population	Killed
El Porvenir	687	553
Velsaya	337	272
Maria del Pilar	1,685	1,335

The list was long and the news sobering. This was the worst of the human tragedies dealt out by Mitch.

The lack of adequate preparation soon became apparent. From Yoro to Choluteca, shortages of food, water and medicine were reported. Rescue teams were undermanned and under-equipped to help the thousands stranded on rooftops or high ground. Telephone service and electricity were down in many communities. And the initial lack of police or military presence in the cities allowed hundreds of looters to ransack unprotected residences and businesses.

A village destroyed by the huge mudslide from Casita Hill. Notice, almost nothing is left except for mud.

We did drive up this ramp but were not able to go farther by vehicle.

The debris was deposited here by the mudslide. This would be just after where the first two villages were destroyed and at the beginning of the creek bed.

NOVEMBER 4, 1999

CHINANDEGA, NICARAGUA–In a desperate effort to stave off disease and starvation, rescuers turned their attention Tuesday from finding the the dead to rescuing the living as the death toll from Hurricane Mitch appeared likely to rise above 13,000.

Grieving relatives jammed morgues and hospitals looking for loved ones.

"We have before us a panorama of death." Honduran President Carlos Flores Facusse said.

Nicaraguan rescuers abandoned efforts to recover up to 2,000 bodies buried under mud after a crater wall of the Casitas Volcano collapsed.

Instead, they're declaring the area a "national cemetery". Those bodies not buried under the mud will be burned to prevent outbreaks of disease, officials said.

"The Red Cross and the (Nicaraguan) army are in the process of rescuing the living, which is the number one priority," Red Cross spokeswoman Leonora Rivera said. "We're not looking for bodies. The dead are dead."

Hundreds of angry Nicaraguans jeered President Arnoldo Aleman because of his perceived lack of relief efforts, calling him "murderer" and begging for food.

Pope John Paul II urged worldwide aid to help Central America. The European Union approved $7.7 million in aid Tuesday.

Eighteen U.S. Blackhawk and Chinook helicopters, four U.S. cargo jets and more than 60 U.S. soldiers and sailors from Panama assisted the Nicaraguan and Honduran armies Tuesday. They plucked villagers from trees and rooftops and delivered food.

Murderous Mudslide

Whole villages on the south slope of Casita were engulfed by the torrent. Thousands died, and images of mutilated corpses and scarred survivors were broadcast almost non-stop on television.

Scenes of horror and destruction filled the front pages of the local daily newspapers. The victims were in shock, as was much of the nation.

People on rooftops waiting to be rescued.

Medical Aid

Health workers in affected zones commented to the press that they were stretched to the limit, attending to unending lines of patients needing treatment at the refugees that have been established.

Healing wounds, issuing antibiotics, treating fungal infestations, giving counsel on treating water before drinking it, assuaging trauma: a multiplicity of tasks calling for a Herculean effort in the midst of chaos.

Nicaraguan doctors, nurses, and health workers on the different scenes of the disaster pushed themselves to their limits.

A nurse treating survivors of the Posoltega mudslide expressed her desire that helicopters ferrying reporters to the scene carry medical supplies instead. More staff was needed, and is needed still.

The Cuban government offered to send doctors and medical supplies to help Nicaragua. President Aleman stated that any amount of medicine that Cuba was willing to donate was more than welcome, but more doctors were not needed. Explaining this to the press, he stated, "As you all know, we have plenty of doctors here." Five months ago, the Health Ministry had released a number of doctors on staff in State-run health facilities due to budget constraints.

Ensuring Aid Delivery

The government watchdog agency, led by Comptroller-General Agustin Jarquin, has a team of auditors checking on the distribution of the aid. They have noted no anomalies, with the exception of some of food aid being sold on the black market. The amount, however, is minor in comparison to the quantities involved.

Nevertheless, there have been some incidents of hoarding and speculation by private merchants manipulating stocks of basic foodstuffs so that prices will rise, bringing higher profits. On November 11, the National Assembly passed the Law for Consumer Defense which gives legal teeth to efforts to put a stop to such corruption in the private sector.

One of the first to fall was a merchant in a Managua market-place who had hidden 300

Floodwaters cover the main road.

100-pound sacks of beans in a veterinary products storeroom, waiting for the price to rise. Rather than confiscating the beans, police forced him to put them up for sale in the market.

Meanwhile, the government announced that it will import 11,000 tons of beans from the United States and 15,000 tons of corn from other countries to offset the shortfall of basic staples caused by the massive destruction of crops all over the country. The hope is that with an abundance of these foodstuffs on the local market, people will not have to pay the higher prices being charged by speculators.

The Clinton administration is proposing that Congress approve more than $950 million in supplemental spending to help Central America and the Eastern Caribbean recover from the devastation wrought last fall by Hurricanes Mitch and Georges.

If approved by Congress, the total U.S. assistance for recovery efforts will exceed $1,200 million "and it will help in several critical ways," Mrs. Clinton said.

"First, 17 million people will have help protecting themselves from the contagious diseases that too often rear their ugly heads in the aftermath of natural disasters. Seven hundred health clinics will be up and running, and more than seven million people will have access to clean water and proper sanitation.

Cars and trucks stranded by high water.

Arrival of a boat, loaded with C.A.M. provisions, at a village on the Ulua River brought excitement and expressions of appreciation from local residents. In fact, the first trip to the villages nearly ended in disaster as anxious and desperate residents rushed the boat–nearly swamping it. After promises that there would be more in the following days and with cooperation from the village presidents, distribution went smoothly from there on. D.S.H.

Roadsigns under water.

Mitch Leaves Nation in Ruins

Printed with permission from *Honduras This Week*.

NOVEMBER 7, 1998

Damage to Infrastructure, Agriculture Estimated in the Billions

TEGUCIGALPA–The skies cleared this week and the sun has come out now and then, allowing Hondurans to get a firsthand look at the extent of the devastation caused by Hurricane Mitch and to begin reconstruction.

And a monumental cleanup and rebuilding task it will be: Aside from the over 6,000 dead and 11,000 missing, nearly 20 percent of the nation's 5.3 million people are homeless or unable to return to their homes due to flooding and as much as 60 percent of the nation's infrastructure, and 70 percent of the crops were destroyed.

No one in their wildest dreams here could have ever imagined the enormous amount of devastation Mitch or any other hurricane for that matter could inflict. True, many people recall Hurricane Fifi, which destroyed North Coast banana plantations and killed an estimated 6,000 people. But that was just the North Coast, the Caribbean, where hurricane damage is expected every once in a while.

This time it was different. After slowly moving west toward Belize and the Yucatan peninsula, Mitch – a rare category 5 hurricane with sustained winds reaching 180 mph on Oct. 27 – suddenly veered south, first pounding the island of Guanaja and then moving onto the Honduran mainland.

Downgraded to a tropical storm, Mitch's still heavy winds and torrential rains wreaked havoc on the fertile Aguan and Sula valleys.

Wake of Ruin

Continuing on its path across the nation, the

No one in their wildest dreams could have ever imagined the enormous damage that a hurricane could inflict.

storm dumped upwards of 40 inches of rain on the unprepared mountainous central and southern departments of Honduras with unprecedented and devastating results.

The lack of adequate preparation soon became apparent. From Yoro to Choluteca, shortages of food, water and medicine were reported. Rescue teams were undermanned and under-equipped to help the thousands stranded on rooftops or high ground. Telephone service and electricity were down in many communities. And the initial lack of police or military presence in the cities allowed hundreds of looters to ransack unprotected residences and businesses.

Stunned by the magnitude of the hurricane, the government began to take drastic steps once the rains had ceased.

Among the measures implemented by the government are:

* The suspension of several constitutional rights for 15 days and a 9 p.m. to 5 a.m. curfew to prevent looting and vandalism;

* Gasoline rationing. Gasoline station hours are 6 a.m. to 6 p.m. and private vehicle owners can purchase no more than Lps. 100 of fuel;

* A price freeze on 32 basic consumer goods, including rice, beans, wheat, corn, meat, vegetable oil, eggs, milk, margarine, orange, plantains, onion, potatoes, tomatoes, sugar, coffee and soap;

* Suspension of classes and the closure of all educational centers, public and private until further notice.

Sections of all major highways were washed out or covered by landslides and fallen trees, making vehicular transportation impossible. On just the recently inaugurated highway between Tegucigalpa and Valle de Angeles, six sections were washed out.

More tragic was the destruction of entire communities and residential districts, such as Morolica in Choluteca department and Guacamaya

The small creek that is hardly visible to the far left in this photo, became a huge, raging river during Hurricane Mitch. What was once part of the city of El Progreso, Yoro, complete with houses and streets is now a rocky river bed. It is not known, exactly, how many houses were washed away with the waters of Mitch in this area. Available space for building houses has also been reduced.

This photo was taken from a street that ended abruptly with a 12 to 15 foot drop to the river bed. It had been a through-street with houses on both sides, connecting with the street on the far side of the photo (just left of center) right of last house visible on the bank.

(between Santa Rita and El Progreso), which were literally wiped off the map by heavy flooding.

In the fruit export industry, one of the nation's principal moneymakers, a Tela Railroad Company official said in a La Tribuna report that 100 percent of his company's banana and African palm plantations were destroyed with losses and damages (including infrastructure) calculated at $850 million.

Foreign aid immediately began pouring in last week, beginning with a US $125,000 donation made by the U.S. government Oct. 28 that has since been raised to $2 million. On Wednesday (Nov. 4), the European Commission announced it was donating 6.8 million ecus (approximately $8 million) in humanitarian aid to the Central American nations affected by Hurricane Mitch, while the Republic of China has donated $800,000 dollars in aid.

In other assistance, Radio America reported that the Cuban government has sent a medical brigade to La Ceiba that will provide medical assistance to hurricane victims in La Mosquitia. Also, crewmen of a British warship are currently helping to reestablish water supply and electric power on the island of Guanaja, where an estimated 2,000 people were left homeless.

Meanwhile, first lad Mary de Flores announced the creation of the Fundacion Maria, a special fund to channel monetary, food and medical assistance to hurricane victims.

Some Good News

However, all the news isn't bad. Roatan escaped relatively unscathed from the hurricane and is now preparing to receive tourists–the island's chief moneymaker.

The maquilas (apparel and assembly plants) in San Pedro Sula and satellite cities were for the most part spared and should be functioning normally soon. Nevertheless, they reported losses of $2 million daily as a result of the storm.

Best of all the El Cajon reservoir has regained its optimal water level, allowing all four generators to work at full capacity and reduce the need for imported oil that is required to run the nation's thermal generators.

More destruction along the road to Tegucigalpa.

Some people made their floors with wooden pallets and others left dirt floors.

Home with more improved siding than most homes now have.

The houses on these pictures show us how they were built, with six cement posts, rafters and metal roofs. The natives enclosed the sides with plastic, sticks, concrete blocks, pallet boards and some used boards that made it look like logs.

 The structures shown are houses being built by volunteers from Belize and the U.S.A. with funding from Christian Aid Ministries. Each house measures 16'x 24' and allows for at least two rooms. Local labor is utilized to assist the volunteers as much as possible. Six eight-inch concrete pillars are poured and left to cure a week or two before framing for the roof is begun. Concrete is all mixed by hand, usually by homeowners, family, neighbors and volunteers. While these houses seem to be small for many Hondurans who live in temporary shelters and tents since Mitch, receiving a "C.A.M. House" is a great privilege.

 When the roof is finished it is left to the homeowner to finish the outside walls as he chooses.

Devastated Mitch Victims Struggle to Recover

Printed with permission from *USA Today*.

NOVEMBER 6, 1998

TEGUCIGALPA, Honduras-Hondurans buried more of their dead Thursday and formed blocks-long lines to get rationed water and gasoline, while officials struggled to feed and shelter a population in shock from Hurricane Mitch.

In Washington, President Clinton ordered that $30 million in Defense Department equipment services and $36 million in food, fuel and other aid be provided to Nicaragua, Honduras, El Salvador and Guatemala immediately.

The White House also announced that Clinton is dispatching Tipper Gore, wife of Vice President Gore, to Central America to show the U.S. commitment to providing humanitarian relief.

First lady Hillary Rodham Clinton also will travel to the region, visiting Nicaragua and Honduras November 16.

"This is the worst disaster we have seen in this hemisphere," said Brian Atwood, head of the Agency for International Development. He said emergency food aid from New Orleans will be sent to the area aboard Boeing 747s, starting Saturday.

The U.N. World Food Program announced it was diverting ships to rush their cargoes of donated food to Central America and was pulling food from warehouses at its base in Rome for delivery by emergency relief flights.

In Tegucigalpa, the capital of Honduras, rescuers began searching for avalanche victims, and decomposed bodies were being buried in common graves.

About 100 victims had been buried so far.

Mayor Castellanos's body is being moved. He was killed in a helicopter crash.

In the flood-ravaged neighborhood of Nueva speranza, Mexican military rescuers, carrying search dogs on their backs, crossed a muddy river to look for people believed buried in a 200-foot avalanche last Friday. Dozens of homes were swept into the river.

"We have receded many years," in terms of development, Honduran President Carlos Flores said. "The capital is in a precarious condition."

Fearing the spread of disease in overcrowded shelters, the government announced plans today to vaccinate shelter refugees against cholera. They also were burning corpses to prevent the spread of disease.

Main highways connecting Tegucigalpa, a city of 800,000, to the rest of the country were cut, creating shortages of gasoline, drinking water and food in the hard-hit capital. Without gasoline, aid can't be delivered by truck. Nearly all aircraft are being used in continuing searches for survivors.

"The people's desperation is growing," said Andres Arguirano Duarte of the emergency committee.

At the city's morgue, operating from a refrigerated trailer after flooding swept through the morgue building, anxious residents awaited word of missing loved ones.

And along the banks of the Choluteca River, residents shoveled muck from debris-packed homes and stores, trying to salvage whatever they could. Bulldozers cleared mounds of rock, mud and garbage from the streets.

All too often, there was nothing left to save.

"How do we continue, without water, without food, without sleep?" said Yolanda Marvella Arraya, 35, who has spent the last week outside on a soggy mattress since flooding destroyed her home.

Also, the Coast Guard said Thursday that it had suspended its search for the Fantome, a historic four-masted schooner that vanished with its 31-member crew nine days ago as deadly Hurricane Mitch bore down on Honduras.

The 282-foot, 128-passenger ship, once owned by Aristotle Onassis, was last heard from October 27.

Nearly all aircraft is being used to search for survivors, and delivering food to stranded people.

Mayor Castellanos Killed in Copter Crash

Printed with permission from *Honduras This Week*.

NOVEMBER 7, 1998

As if the devastation left by Hurricane Mitch wasn't enough bad news, Tegucigalpa residents were dealt a second blow with the unexpected death of popular Mayor Cesar Castellanos.

Fondly known as "El Gordito," Castellanos and three others died in a helicopter crash last Sunday (Nov. 1) shortly after takeoff from Toncontin International Airport.

Also killed in the crash were Maj. Jose Miranda, the pilot; Arturo Calona, a city employee; and Geovany Sanchez, a cameraman.

Coincidently, it was Castellanos' birthday.

Council Nahum Valladares, is expected to succeed Castellanos as mayor of the twin cities.

MARCH, 1999

China To Pay for Chopper

The government of the Republic of China will pick up the US $3.5 million (Lps. 50 million) tab of the new helicopter recently acquired by the Honduran government for use by the presidency, the Daily El Heraldo reported Saturday (Jan. 30).

Government funds set aside for the helicopter's purchase, which was made before Hurricane Mitch hit Honduras, will now be used for housing projects and relief assistance.

The decision to acquire a new helicopter was made for safety reasons, given the close calls that former Presidents Callejas and Reina had in old military helicopters. Subsequent to the decision, Mayor Castellanos and three others died in the crash of a military helicopter last Novemberr.

A picture of helicopter crash were Mayor Cesar Castellanos was killed on November 1, 1998 after take-off from Toncontin International Airport.

Unprecedented Show of Support for Honduras

Printed with permission from *Honduras This Week*

Tens of Thousands Left Homeless in Wake of Hurricane's Destruction

TEGUCIGALPA–The fate of five servicemen stationed on Swan Island and residents of Guanaja and parts of Roatan, which were hit hard by the hurricane, is uncertain.

The storm revealed just how unprepared Honduras is for natural disasters, and has conjured up memories of Hurricane Fifi that devastated the North Coast in 1974.

The greatest damage has occurred along the Atlantic coast in the departments of the Bay Islands, Cortes, Atlantida, Colon, Yoro and Gracias a Dios.

The area most affected has been the island of Guanaja, where more than 80 percent of the buildings have reportedly been destroyed while the roofs of shelters holding more than a thousand persons were blown off by strong winds.

In Roatan, the largest of the Bay islands, electricity is out, airports are flooded and there has been enormous environmental damage.

Men, women and children traveled through dirty water carrying supplies and whatever goods they could salvage from their devastated homes. People working in groups became something that was seen everywhere. Everyone shared whatever they had.

Worse than any snowstorm, digging out of the mud in the weeks following Mitch was not only labor intensive; it was messy. The man, attempting to clean out his driveway with the tractor-loader seemed to be fighting a loosing battle with mud. This scene was photographed in the town of La Lima, a short distance east of San Pedro Sula, in northern Honduras on November 10, 1998.

Notice the crosses over the gravesite. Many people were buried where they were found.

This is a curve in the creek bed. There was a road that cut off to the right at this curve.

About 40 bridges in Nicaragua did not survive. This bridge did, although the approaches to the bridge on both sides were washed out. The Nicaraguan government put in temporary bridges to detour these. Along the Pan American Highway most bridges were affected either with damage to the bridge itself or to the approaches.

President Flores and First Lady Send SOS to the World

Printed with permission from Honduras This Week

NOVEMBER 7, 1998

"Honduras is mortally wounded but not in agony," stated President Flores when he asked for solidarity with the thousands of dead, wounded and homeless as a result of Hurricane Mitch.

Before the nation on national and international radio and television, Flores made a desperate call for Hondurans affected by the national disaster caused by heavy rains and flooding.

"It's obvious to all Honduran residents that we are facing a national disaster of historic proportions that in some parts of the country can be considered a public calamity," he said.

"The information we have been able to gather presents a panorama of death, desolation and destruction nationwide. There is almost no place in Honduras that has not been touched. This pathetic data will most assuredly increase with access to several places still isolated and as soon as it is possible to conclude evacuation.

"Overflowing rivers and landslides have caused complete barrios to disappear even though extensive preventive efforts were made for early evacuations, but still not all the affected were able to be saved; many victims have for more than five days sat on the roofs of their homes, without food, exposed to the weather, waiting to be rescued.

"Bodies are everywhere, victims of landslides and the waters. The most conservative calculations estimate thousands not hundreds of deaths. Many municipal governments have begun to run out of food and potable water. The capital of Republic is in a disastrous, calamitous situation. On top of it all, the death of Tegucigalpa Mayor Dr. Cesar Castellanos in a fatal helicopter accident while working with relief efforts has left citizens desolate. Dr. Castellanos was an exemplary, diligent, and dynamic leader, much help had been placed in him for the reordering and reconstruction of the city. Now, the best tribute that we can give Dr. Castellanos is to follow his plans for a new capital.

"A few minutes ago, in the Council of Ministers, we agreed to take extraordinary measures, destined to exercise control over the situation, avoid looting and vandalism and put the severely damaged national life into order bit by bit.

"Although some constitutional rights will be temporarily suspended, individual freedom, freedom of press, freedom to associate and meet, and all rights pertaining to the inherent liberty of the citizenry to work, reconstruct their own lives and collaborate in the emergency tasks and normalization activities are guaranteed.

"We are making an urgent call to the international community, to sister governments and friends, financial and aid organizations."

There is almost no place in Honduras that has not been touched by death, desolation and destruction.

U.S. Military Based in Honduras Participating in Relief Efforts

Printed with permission from *Honduras This Week*.

NOVEMBER 7, 1998

SOTO CANO AIR BASE–"Auxilio, auxilio por favor," was faintly screeched by abandoned children as helicopters hovered over the city of Tunga.

"Gracia por salvar a nuestros ninos," cried family and friends to the helicopter crew as children were dropped off and reunited with loved ones.

Heavy winds and rains causing floods and mudslides from Hurricane Mitch have left many people along the Northern coast of Honduras without shelter, power and food.

Due to numerous flight reconnaissance missions conducted, Company D, 228th Aviation Regiment, Joint Task Force-Bravo, rescued several children who were trapped on top of houses due to flooding, as well as air dropped nearly 100 cases of meals-ready-to-eat and blankets to hunger stricken areas Nov. 1.

Four UH-60 Black Hawk helicopters were sent to areas of La Ceiba, San Pedro Sula, Tunga, and Trujillo Bay to conduct observations of damage and provide humanitarian assistance where needed.

"Our full scale, long range goal has become providing immediate disaster relief operations throughout Honduras as well as other parts of Central America," he said.

According to Chief Warrant Officer 2 Richard Lindsford, Co. D. 228th Aviation Reg., UH-60 pilot, the mission was a success and he was proud to be part of it.

"We helped many children get back to their families safely," he said. "It's great to be part of such humanitarian efforts, especially when you see the good we're doing and how the people of Honduras react to our help."

According to Sgt. Vincent Conyers, Co. D, 228th Aviation Reg., flight paramedic, the people we helped couldn't stop thanking us.

Water almost reaches the peak of the roof where three people are waiting to be rescued.

French President Chirac Visits Tegucigalpa

Printed with permission from *Honduras This Week*.

NOVEMBER 7, 1998

TEGUCIGALPA—French President Jacques Chirac on Monday (Nov. 16) paid a short visit to Tegucigalpa to get a first-hand look at the devastation caused by Hurricane Mitch and to offer his nation's support for the reconstruction of Honduras.

Following a brief tour of several flood-ravaged neighborhoods, Chirac gave a press conference in which he expressed his admiration for the Honduran people who, after being so severely battered by flooding, still stand tall and are willing to work hard to rebuild their country.

Chirac, the first ever French president to visit Honduras, also announced bilateral debt relief in the order of US$120 million dollars, adding that his country will lobby for multilateral debt relief on behalf of Honduras and for the participation of the European Union in the reconstruction and development of Central America.

A meeting of the ministers of cooperation and development is scheduled to be held Nov. 30 and Chirac is of the opinion that for aid relief to be efficient and generous it should be well coordinated.

During the meeting, Chirac expressed his condolences to all the inhabitants of Honduras, especially those who had lost relatives. He offered France's friendship and solidarity as well as their desire to help as much as possible.

"I was extremely impressed with what I saw in Tegucigalpa, especially the looks and smiles on the young faces. You can tell that no one wants to bend under this crisis and the people will continue on their march forward with help from others."

President Flores thanked the French president for taking the time from his busy schedule to visit Honduras personally. He said, "France has shown invaluable leadership for our cause, which is vitally important in the reconstruction of Honduras."

Airport under water.

Residents of Decimated Barrio Miramesi Make Plans for the Future

Printed with permission from *Honduras This Week*.

NOVEMBER 7, 1998

TEGUCIGALPA–Hurricane Mitch wiped out four communities in the capital. Among these the riverbank community of Miramesi of approximately 1,000 people was completely displaced.

Residents say that during the dawn of Saturday (Oct. 31), flood waters forced them to higher ground three times before they could climb no further. From this final high point they decided to abandon the area, cutting across a coffee field to find access to El Chile Bridge that leads into Tegucigalpa.

Unfortunately the bridge was also covered with water and several people were washed off. The timely arrival of Boy Scout Leader German Rivera and his troop of scouts proved a godsend. The scouts were able to pull out the people hanging on the bridge and no one perished. German had been watching the situation from across the river and realized that the people would need help.

Many of the inhabitants had resided in the area for more than 20 years.

After the initial shock of being homeless wore off and basic food, water, and shelter needs were taken care, Miramesi residents have started to organize and look to the future with the help of relief volunteer Michael Miller. Miller is volunteer supported by the Presbyterian Church.

The close-knit community has decided to stay together and is currently thinking about starting a micro-enterprise to finance the construction of New Miramesi in another location. They have organized themselves into three committees toward this end: one will approach the mayor's office about land, another will raise funds, and a third will be in charge of organizing and communicating with the people of Miramesi.

Motivation and spirits are high. They feel if they stick together there is hope for the future.

Road sign to El Progreso under water.

Debris on the electric wires is physical evidence of the height of the flooding creeks and rivers in this scene in Tegucigalpa. Once a bustling business center, many streets on November 14, 1998 seemed deserted, except for clean-up crews.

Another home being built by C.A.M.

Hurricane Mitch Wrings Destruction On Tegucigalpa

Printed with permission from *Honduras This Week.*

NOVEMBER 7, 1998

TEGUCIGALPA–After hovering over the North Coast of Honduras for three days causing extensive damage and irreplaceable loss, Hurricane Mitch moved south.

Before reaching the Tegucigalpa area the hurricane converted into a tropical storm that veered west of the city, thus sparing the capital ferocious winds.

However, heavy rains caused rivers flowing through the city to overflow and caused an unprecedented path of destruction during the early hours of Saturday (Oct. 31). Flooding and mudslides resulted in a general collapse of basic infrastructure.

Along the banks of the Rio Choluteca four barrios disappeared completely. Hundreds of homes and buildings were lost and key bridges swept away, causing serious communication problems within the city and with other parts of the country.

But property loss cannot be only attributed to flood waters. Well organized vandals ransacked affected market areas using trucks to tote off looted merchandise. Gunshots in the night roused a sense of general anarchy.

Hurricane Mitch causes extensive damage and irreplaceable loss.

Environmental Disregard Nicaragua Pays the Price

Printed with permission from an adaption by *La Prensa*.

NOVEMBER 9, 1998

Nature is charging Nicaragua for its history of environmental disregard. Mountain slopes in Nicaragua, laid bare by deforestation and burned in the fires (in April and May) this year, lost the natural protection provided by forest cover. With Hurricane Mitch, they could not contain the avalanche of water running down slopes, opening up torrential spillways, swelling hundreds of rivers, unleashing mudslides, flooding plains, valleys, and lowlands.

Last dry season, satellite images showed there were over 18,000 forest fires in Nicaragua, more than all the fires at that time in the rest of Central America and more than all the forest fires in the last 8 years in Nicaragua.

When the deluge of Mitch happened, the water was not retained and absorbed by the soil. It ran off over the surface, opening gullies, making rivers overflow their banks. Rivers ran rampant, the currents destroying bridges, roads, and farm fields. Mudslides buried hamlets and families in a way never before seen in Nicaragua.

Signs that a disaster like this might happen have been clear in recent years with the repetitive flooding that occurs —especially in certain zones with clayey soils crossed by rivers from deforested drainage basins, like the Rio Negro basin in northern Chinandega.

This year, the northwest was hit the worst. The plains were deforested extensively during the cotton boom. More recently, the forests at the foot and on the skirts of the Maribios volcano chain have been cleared.

The forests have also been cleared in the central mountains, as well as in the Dipilto and Jalapa highlands where the pine forests have almost disappeared.

A family escaping the high waters by boat.

This is – or rather was – a well-to-do housing development in Tegucigalpa. The land shifted and caused buildings to collapse and fall into the flooded river below.

These are a few houses severely damaged in the mudslide. You can see the remains of a foundation in the bottom right corner of the photo. Some of these people plan to rebuild, but others have left to go live in Tegucigalpa.

University Providing Shelter to Thousands

Printed with permission from *Honduras This Week*.

NOVEMBER 14, 1998
Harsh Situation

When I came inside the room, Igancia, a young woman of 22, stood up and walked toward me as if she wanted to say something, but didn't. Instead, she returned to her chair and sat there while looking at me silently. I explained to her I wanted to conduct an interview, and perhaps the chance of being taken note of in the middle of all those thousands of people encouraged her to come forward.

"I come from la Colonia Villa Nueva, Sector 2, do you know where is it?" she told me. "Well, our house had sunk in the edge of the ravine. We lost all our possessions, we get a little bread and a cup of coffee. I give a little bit of bread to my kid next to me because babies and little kids won't get milk until the next day at ten. That's about it. I spend most of the time taking care of my babies while by husband is working to help clean up Comayaguela."

Ignacia's example is not necessarily representative of the people here. The level of suffering being endured varies, depending on the different conditions; some families may have lost just a couple pieces of furniture, others their home, while others have lost someone in their family.

In general, one of the volunteers explained, "They feel very lonely and abandoned, some of them demand too much attention. Some others none at all. There are also many personal conflicts between the families that have to share the same classroom that has been assigned to them. Some classrooms have as few as two and others as many as six or seven families inside."

He added, "At the Departments of Psychology

Houses collapsed at the edge of a ravine.

and Social Work, we began to observe that there are many cases of neurosis, collective hysteria and many cases of severe depression, especially among women. This is not helped by some of the people working here, who perhaps have become a little too insensitive, yelling and speaking to them in a very harsh tone of voice that may intimidate them, and prevent them from asking for the things they need or from expressing their feelings."

Organization

As important as it has been helping the flood victims to more or less cover their basic needs, it is even more important to consider how to reintegrate them back into society.

The first step was to put everybody to work, with the creation of organizational groups inside each room, where women must clean the halls, the classrooms and the bathrooms, wash their clothes and cook their own meals.

Every floor has a supervisor or coordinator, who is in charge of making a head count in each room and to verify that people are getting what they really need. He or she must also communicate any major problems to the social workers and nurses at the shelter.

To help maintain order, records are kept on how many people live in each building. But this is not an easy task, since some families have left after two or three days, while new families continue to arrive.

The process of making head counts may sound easy, but for some reason numbers are never exact or definitive. Four buildings provide shelter to victims. The first one had 136 people, the second 394, the third and the fourth couldn't give the exact number, but as could be easily seen, the number of people in the last two buildings was much greater.

At the beginning, there was an estimated 5,000 flood victims, but the amount has dropped 40 percent for various reasons. Some families returned to their homes after they realized they could live in them again. Others lost their homes, but received help from close friends or relatives. Still others simply preferred to go to the streets and look for a better opportunity.

Many homes were flooded by the high water.

World Leaders Continue to Express Their Solidarity

Printed with permission from *Honduras This Week*.

NOVEMBER 16, 1998

TEGUCIGALPA—Current and former world leaders continue to express their solidarity to Hondurans and promising assistance for the reconstruction of the nation, which was recently devastated by Hurricane Mitch.

The first international figure to arrive was former U.S. President George Bush. Prince Philip of Spain is expected to arrive today and President Jacques Chirac of France—the first ever by a French head of state—and U.S. first lady Hillary Clinton are scheduled to arrive on Monday.

On Tuesday (Nov. 10), Tipper Gore, the wife of U.S. Vice President Al Gore, visited the capital to survey the damage caused by the hurricane, the deadliest hurricane in the Caribbean in more than 200 years. "The world must know that the tragedy in Central America is one of biblical proportions," said Mrs. Gore after observing the damage firsthand.

Mrs. Gore traveled with a U.S. delegation that included Senators Christopher Dodd (D-CT), Jeff Bingaman (D-NM), and Mary Landrieu (D-LA); Reps. Gary Ackerman (D-NY)l Jim Kolbe (R-AZ), and Xavier Becerra (D-CA); USAID Director Brian Atwood; Principal Deputy Assistant Secretary of State for InterAmerican Affairs Jack Leonard; and Atlanta Braves star Dennis Martinez.

Previously, former President George Bush toured the capital on Sunday (Nov. 6) and came away astounded by the magnitude of damage caused by the flooding. Initially, Bush accompanied by President Flores, visited the El Chile Barrio, La Concordia and the Honduran Social Security Hospital in Barrio Abajo. Based on his observations, Bush will make recommendations to the U.S. government about the best way to provide assistance.

Meanwhile, France this week announced it was pardoning Honduras' debt.

A child being rescued by boat.

These photos taken along the San Pedro Sula, El Progreso Highway, show some of the effect on agriculture and the long-term economic effect on the country.

Many Hondurans found employment with the sugar companies and fruit plantations. While much of the sugar cane was stunted but survived, bananas, pineapple and other crops did not fair so well. Most banana companies faced one-year of reconditioning groves (restoring irrigation systems, etc.) and another year till first harvest.

For many, this will be two years of hardship and unemployment. D.S.H.

Saying Goodbye To Their Homes Which Was Once The Town Called Miramesi

Printed with permission from *Honduras This Week*.

NOVEMBER 16, 1998

Florencia Aguilar took me by the hand and led me down the banks of the Choluteca River, the same river that destroyed a large portion of Tegucigalpa a week ago. With sad, yet infinitely patient eyes, she pointed to the middle of the stream and said, "Michael, that is where my family lived for almost twelve years."

She proceeded to tell me about how last Saturday night, as the waters quickly rose up to her doorstep and into her small house, her terrorized family grabbed everything they could and ran. Yet within minutes, they as well as the rest of the Miramesi neighborhood, were waist-deep in mud and rushing water, They dropped everything they were trying to take with them and escaped with their lives.

As Florencia and I slowly walked through what was once Miramesi, dodging man-sized boulders that rolled like giant wrecking balls down the river and into Miramesi, Florencia suddenly stopped. "Look Michael," she said, picking up a small, muddy shirt. "This shirt belonged to my son." Her dark eyes seemed to grow deeper and a shade sadder.

We came back to Miramesi this week with the whole community. Raul Reyes, the young president of the community association, and I decided that the community needed to say a collective goodbye to its long-time home.

At 10 am Monday morning, we gathered at the Plaza of the old Los Dolores Church in downtown Tegucigalpa. When 500 people arrived, we began a procession, a pilgrimage really, down to the edge of the river where Miramesi once stood. As we got closer, the walking became more difficult. We had to detour around the rubble of buildings and broken, stooped power lines.

Florence Aguilar took me by the hand and led me down the banks of the Choluteca River, the same river that destroyed a large portion of Tegucigalpa a week ago. With sad, yet infinitely patient eyes she pointed to the middle of the stream and said, "Michael, that is where my family lived for almost 12 years."

As we turned the corner and began the descent into Miramesi, a hush worked its way down the line of people walking down the broken road. Then, upon entering the community, I began to hear, "Look, this is where my house used to be!" "Hey, I think that's Maria's old bicycle!" "Isn't that part of the sign that hung in front of Chemo's old store?"

Some people cried in each other's arms, while others, with little fatalistic smiles, tried to make small, quiet jokes about their fate. "Hey, you just walked into my living room without knocking," I overheard one old man joke to a long-time friend as they stood on a broken cement foundation.

After allowing the community some time to reflect on what was, we called the people together to begin to talk about what will be. Standing amidst the rubble of their old lives, we asked the community to allow the past to be the foundation stone for the future. We asked that just as the river washed away their homes, that they allow it to also wash away old battles, gossip and division.

We spent an hour taking a list of names of people who wanted to rebuild together. We talked of our plans to go to the mayor and ask for land to rebuild the community as a whole. I spoke of the generous support the people are receiving from my community in the United States.

But the people of Miramesi do not want to be receivers only. They want to take an active role in rebuilding their community. One old man took off his cowboy hat and began to pass it around. After it had gone through everyone's hands, the community had raised 600 lempiras, almost 50 dollars, to help itself rebuild. Each lempira given was a sacrifice on the part of families that have nothing and a symbol of the unity on which the community stands.

Raul asked me to give the last word to the community. As I spoke to them in their last moments in the old community, I held up a copy of Honduras This Week. The community had been featured in the newspaper the day before. I told them that the newspaper presented them as a unified, hope-filled people who are willing to work to rebuild their lives. "Is this true?" I asked. "Si," they shouted back. Then, from the back a man shouted, "Que viva Neueva Miramesi!" "Long live the New Miramesi!" With one voice, the entire community took up the cheer.

We asked that, "Just as the river washed away their homes, that they allow it to also wash away old battles, gossip, and division."

Again, in Valle De Angels, we see water lines with ground and foundations washed away supported here with poles. A "make-do" still useful six weeks following the visit of Mitch.

Taken from the Pan American Highway. We are about 10-12 miles from the mountain at this point.

Skin fungi and other cases of foot disease increased dramatically after Mitch, according to reports from doctors and clinics around the country. When boots are not available, or at least not worn, as in this scene in La Lima, the only surprise is that disease is not more rampant.

While many small stores and shops were quickly cleaned out and restocked by November 11, 1998, it was still far from "business as usual." The mud and debris in the street in front of these stores in La Lima are evidence of the difficulties still facing these businesses.

Patuca Residents Hardhit by Flooding

Printed with permission from *Honduras This Week*

DECEMBER 12, 1998

PICHOLO, Olancho–All along the Rio Patuca the story is the same: "The river rose 20, 30, 40 feet during tropical storm Mitch and washed all our possessions away."

Indigenous peoples and Ladino colonists who make their living as subsistence farmers, cattle ranchers and gold panners all suffered losses, some more than others. The subsistence farmers were the hardest hit, the loss of their homes they mourn less than their food crops. Crops of corn, beans and manioc planted on the riverbanks were totally destroyed, as the topsoil washed away leaving barren bedrock in its place.

Help is a long time coming and many are having trouble finding food. Those who have share with those who don't.

Don Ricardo, an intelligent, and optimistic man, said in a shy voice, "Now I'm a *damnificado* (flood victim)." Don Ricardo had his camp and three gold panning machines on the Rio Patuca when the storm hit. Now he is camped on the Cuyamel River in a pair of plastic shacks.

When he invited me in for some coffee and a meal of rice, beans and wild pig, I asked him if the people there were his family. He said, "Not by blood, but we live and work together and that makes us a family, we all take care of each other."

Don Ricardo is also planning to sell one of his gold panning machines to another inhabitant of the Patuca who lost both of his, and who was at that moment in Catacamas selling the last of his livestock (five pigs) to come up with the money.

Leadership qualities such as those displayed by Don Ricardo are not rare in this area. Many of the people are immigrants from the deforested Choluteca regions.

The river rose up to 40 feet during Hurricane Mitch, and washed all their possessions away.

Hondurans at Crossroads: Reconstruct or Create a New Nation

Printed with permission from *Honduras This Week*

DECEMBER 12, 1998

One month has passed since Hurricane Mitch wrought widespread destruction in Honduras and the question remains: In what manner will the country recover from the devastation it has suffered? I believe that Hondurans now face a crucial choice.

The first option is to reconstruct the nation as it existed before the hurricane. Specifically, it would be dangerously easy to reestablish systems that only perpetuate the widespread poverty and ubiquitous socio-economic inequality that have plagued the country since its inception.

The superior alternative is to take advantage of this opportunity to construct a new reality for the future of all Hondurans. By creating policies and programs that promote the true development of the nation's wealth of human and natural resources, Honduras has the ability to emerge from this tragedy as a more democratic, egalitarian, and unified country than ever before.

As a Fulbright Scholar studying development in Honduras, I have been amazed by the country's cultural and ecological diversity, as well as its tremendous potential for human development. Honduras is not only blessed with a variety of natural resources but also with citizens who have the capacity to promote the development of their own country.

Despite the nation's positive attributes, however, daily life in Honduras has taught me that the country grapples with an enigmatic paradox. For although Honduras has all the necessary resources to enable it to become a nation of great wealth, it has historically been a country handicapped by rampant poverty. In order to overcome this fundamental defect and its many related inequalities, Honduras must invest in

City streets are covered by water.

human development, including education, health, women's empowerment, and natural resource protection programs.

One of the most fundamental components of human development is education. In order for a nation to maximize its capabilities, it is necessary to empower its citizens with education. Therefore, Honduras must establish programs throughout the country that promote educational opportunities at the primary and secondary school levels for both girls and boys, as well as literacy programs for adults. Schools should provide students with the skills necessary to enable them to achieve their individual potential and thereby contribute to the development of Honduras.

Another factor that is integral to the full development of Honduras is the promotion of health services. Although diarrhea and malnutrition are entirely avoidable evils, they are currently the leading causes of death among children under five in Honduras.

Consequently, teaching families about sanitation and nutrition and vaccinating children would significantly ameliorate the critical state of public health in Honduras.

IHT Issues Report on Impact of Hurricane Damage

The Honduran Tourism Institute has issued a communique summing up the impact of Hurricane Mitch on the nation's major tourism destinations and, not expected Guanaja – where Mitch stalled for 30 hours – was one of the most devastated sites.

Inland, IHT said the hardest hit areas were Tegucigalpa and the San Pedro Sula area. "Tegucigalpa suffered greatly when heavy rains collapsed a neighborhood into the Choluteca River, forming a lake that inundated the downtown area. Most of the bridges in Tegucigalpa were destroyed (or seriously damaged) in the flood and many lives were lost. Tegucigalpa was cut off from the rest of the country by damage to roads and bridges."

IHT said, "The lodging facilities have risen to the occasion, serving the thousands of relief workers and international press as they poured into the country in response to the crisis. The infrastructure of basic services like electricity and water survived with some damage, and the city is

Most of this bridge has been washed away by high waters.

working to clean up. Traffic is likely to be an issue for some time with the number of missing bridges. Access to nearby tourism destinations, such as Valle de Angeles and Santa Lucia, has been restored."

In the San Pedro Sula Area, widespread flooding destroyed much of the agricultural base of the region, IHT said. "The international airport was flooded, damaging some of the electronic equipment used in communicating with aircraft."

Meanwhile, a ship with 31 crewmembers remained missing Sunday, five days after it was last heard from while it was trying to evade Hurricane Mitch. Extensive searches for the Fantome uncovered no trace of the 282-foot sailing ship used by Miami-based Windjammer Barefoot Cruises.

Trujillo, to the west of La Ceiba, was closer to the point where the eye of Mitch came ashore and sustained significant damage to vegetation. "Significant amount of debris have accumulated on the beaches. While some lodging facilities suffered minor damage, almost all are open and ready for visitors."

"Approaching La Ceiba," continued the report, "one begins to move into more highly impacted areas. The Cangrejal River flooded badly, destroying some houses and at least temporarily halting white water rafting. Some trees were reported down in Pico Bonito National Park. There is a great deal of storm debris blown up onto the beaches. Most lodging facilities are open and serving guests, although some are repairing minor damage."

Trujillo, to the west of La Ceiba, was closer to the point where the eye of Mitch came ashore and sustained significant damage to vegetation. "Significant amounts of debris have accumulated on the beaches. While some lodging facilities suffered minor damage, almost all are open and ready for visitors."

Raging flood waters pound these buildings and streets.

U.S. Military Supports Relief Efforts in Olancho

Printed with permission from *Honduras This Week*.

JANUARY 2, 1999

CATACAMAS–As relief efforts in Honduras continue, methods are being developed to more efficiently distribute supplies to the people who need them most.

One of those methods is the "hub and spoke" system, which Joint Task Force-Bravo has implemented in various parts of Honduras. One such place is the Honduran town of Catacamas.

Catacamas, located in the Department of Olancho, is serving as a "hub" for relief delivery operations throughout the region. Food, medicine and clothes are delivered to the hub via truck and helicopter, and are sorted out depending on what the needs of the "spoke" villages are.

Once it is determined which villages need what supplies by Honduran officials, CH-47 Chinook helicopters from Company C, 159th Aviation Regiment and UH-60 Blackhawk helicopters from Company D, 228th Aviation Regiment, fly relief missions to the villages and then return to the hub for their next mission.

Hub & Spoke/2-2-2

"We fly from Soto Cano to Aguacate, the airstrip outside Catacamas, in the morning and pick up supplies. Once the supplies are loaded, we fly them to whatever village they need to go to. Then, it's back to Aguacate and we continue this round robin delivery system until the end of the day," said Capt. Lori Turbak, a CH-47 pilot.

Hub & Spoke/3-3-3

Although delivering supplies is the main mission of the hub, anything they can do to help the Hondurans in the area they will do. One such instance was the Medevac of a Honduran woman who was in need of medical care.

"We found a lady in one of the villages who was seriously ill and in need of medical attention. We put her and her husband on the helicopter and flew them back to Catacamas."

Supplies being taken to the flood victims by boat.

New and used car dealerships, bus companies, trucking firms, taxis, heavy equipment dealerships and others were also victims of the raging Choluteca River in Tegucigalpa. The truck chassis and bus body seen on the river bed were deposited here from some distance away. These photos give some idea of the millions of dollars lost by businesses and of the overall economic impact on the country. D.S.H.

Hurricane Mitch
A Personal View

Printed with permission from *Honduras This Week.*

JANUARY 9, 1999

Two weeks after the catastrophe, I took a trip to Tegucigalpa. Most of the rubble of the landslides had been cleared. At one point a large portion of the road had fallen away, though we could pass in single file, but it looked like the rest could go at any time. So the bus got through to the river where the bridge had been washed away. The concrete pillars scattered like feathers down the water. We got out and into a wooden box that was dragged by rope across the river, then out and into a bus on the other side.

Arriving in Tegucigalpa, the damage took my breath away. Streets where not long before I had gone walking were a mess of smashed houses, tons of sludge and small rivers. It was hard to remember where the river had originally been. There was a huge lake in the center, half a hillside collapsed, and the walls of houses twisted and tossed about like bits of scrunched-up paper.

Given the epidemic corruption that exists in Honduras, I wonder how much of the aid will get through.

If international agencies, insist on overseeing deliveries, as apparently Christian Aid is doing, there is a good chance it will. Still, one friend visiting an emergency shelter after 3 weeks found that although food was being delivered, they are still wearing the same clothes that they had been wearing the day they had lost everything. An Italian aid worker told me she found things very disorganized, and maybe that is the problem as much as corruption. Honduras is not a well organized country at the best of times and just does not have the infrastructure to administer disaster relief. Still, Hondurans are inured to disaster anyway; it's practically a way of life. But disease and epidemics are a real threat and already happening. Many countries, especially Cuba, are providing extensive health support but it remains to be seen if they can stave off the health calamity that seems to be impending.

Man taken across the river in a wooden box that was dragged by a rope.

Honduran Calamity Draws International Response

Printed with permission from *USA Today*.

NOVEMBER 11, 1998

COMAYAGUELA, HONDURAS–Tana Wooten anchors the rope so Paul Jennings can shimmy down the embankment. Both Americans wear face masks to shield them from the stench. They claw through the mud for hours, hoping that this time, they'll find a lifeless body to give to grieving family members.

Overhead, U.S. soldiers fly to isolated villages, ferrying badly needed food, clothes and medicine.

Farther north, in the Aguan Valley, Keith Rose, a doctor from Texas, goes house-to-house treating sick people.

In the Honduran capital, Vice President Gore's wife, Tipper, sleeps in a tent outside a shelter to show solidarity with the hundreds of thousands of Hondurans who lost their homes.

Back in the USA, Americans jam phone lines at relief agencies asking what they can do to help.

Everyone is up to his knees in mud trying to help Honduras recover from the terrible devastation that was Hurricane Mitch. And those who aren't wish they were.

"There's been a real outpouring of empathy, followed by voluntary aid," says U.S. Ambassador to Honduras James Creagan, who has donated some of his old t-shirts and shoes to the homeless of Honduras.

Hugh Palmer, U.S. Coordinator for Disaster Relief Operations, says he ran into five U.S. Peace Corps volunteering near a smashed bridge in the Honduran capital, Tegucigalpa. The Peace Corps had evacuated its staff last week because of concerns over the deteriorating health in the Central American country, but they wanted to find out how they could stay and help. Several volunteers, he said, have resigned rather than leave.

Searching for the dead with the help of dogs.

Americans like Tana Wooten, a 32-year-old former U.S. servicewoman from Kuna, Idaho, are volunteering their time to help the devastated Hondurans.

Wooten, her husband, Riley, and Paul Jennings go out looking for bodies every day from dawn to dusk in and around the Honduran capital as volunteers with the Tegucigalpa fire brigade.

"We're trying to give the families closure by bringing home the bodies of their loved ones," said Jennings, a 29-year-old Gulf War veteran from Tauton, Mass. "They've been through so much already."

Their team, which also includes two Canadian volunteers and two Honduran firefighters, dig through up to 12 feet of mud looking for corpses.

Jennings carries ropes, gloves, hooks, a helmet and rations. He also lugs heavy trauma equipment for emergency care, even though he says there's no chance of finding survivors any longer.

The American-Canadian team is the main body recovery group working in the capital. But the job is frustrating. Even working 12-hour days, they've only found four bodies since starting last Friday.

"We're getting people calling us saying there's a body here, a body part there," said Riley Wooten, from Fredonia, Kan. "We dig for hours, but we don't find anything. We're wasting a lot of valuable time on false reports. Its the stink that confuses them. People can't distinguish between the stench of animal flesh and human flesh."

The job is also dangerous. "The ground is still very wet and unstable," said Tana as she rubbed cream on a nasty skin rash she has developed on her right forearm.

"We can smell the bodies, but often we just can't get to them. But we're not taking any chances. You don't want a man to die getting a dead body. When the river goes down, we'll be able to get more."

Americans, of course, are not only the ones shouldering the grim duties. Thousands of Hondurans, wearing plastic bags around their feet for shoes, work tirelessly to clear the quicksand-like mud from the gutted shops and buildings in the commercial area of

Heavy equipment is used to dig a trench and bury the dead.

Comayaguela, a suburb of the capital. Homeless men from the shelters spend their days cleaning up the capital.

And it's not only American aid helping to feed the hungry Hondurans either.

Mexican planes fly every day to isolated villages, delivering food and clothing. "The Mexican government has been very generous for a country not nearly as rich as we are," said Parmer, USAID.

British Marines are working along a rip-straddling Honduras and Nicaragua, attempting to reach stranded Native Indians there. Other European countries have joined in the international aid effort. United Nations agencies are also active.

The aid is almost too much for the country to handle. U.S. officials say Honduran authorities are having trouble coordinating the countries and groups wanting to send help.

But the Honduran government worries about how much help they'll get from the international community in the later, and more arduous, task rebuilding the infrastructure and economy of the shattered country. Paying off its foreign debt is a big problem. Honduras owes 4.2 billion and Nicaragua owes $6 billion, mainly to international lending agencies.

U.S. Ambassador James Creagan says the United States "will have a major role (in Honduras) beyond the food."

But the truth is many hard-pressed countries -- from Indonesia to Russia to several African nations -- will soon be clamoring for U.S. aid and volunteers.

In the meantime, Tana Wooten spends her days waist-deep in mud, clawing for bodies.

"I'm staying," said Wooten, who is also a paramedic. "In the States, people like me are a dime a dozen. Here, I feel like I'm really needed."

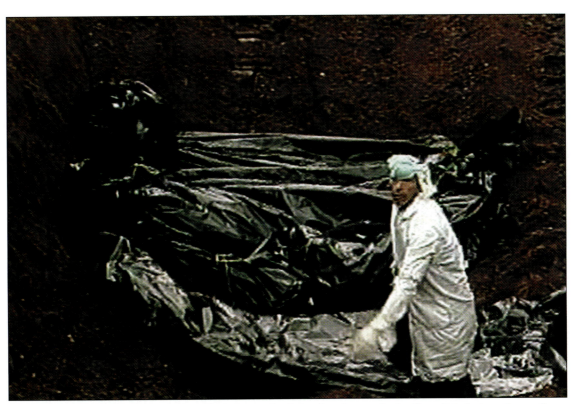

"We're trying to give the families closure by bringing home the bodies of their loved ones."

Another view taken from the bridge between the two cities when my sister, Norma Jean and Kathleen, visited me during the Christmas Season. They brought bracelets, erasers, trinkets, candy, etc., as Christmas cheer for children at the orphanage. One would like to do much more for these people whose lives were most difficult even before the floods. Now it is more barren than before.

This is looking toward the "old city" of Comayaguela. Center front shows some brick construction washed into the river by the storm. – from who-knows-where? The Choluteca River runs between Comayaguela and Tegucigalpa which are located close to one another. This photo was taken from a bridge.

Amid the mud piles and ruins in this photo taken in the old city (Comayaguela) stands a little boy (right center), crying and rubbing his eyes. One feels so sorry for him and for countless others. Everything is gone, home, family, friends…their few precious possessions buried. Digging themselves out may often be the only way to rid oneself of some frustration and anger. These houses were built on the mountain side facing Tegucigalpa.

These were homes in Tegucigalpa, the capital city, which lies over 900 meters (about 3,000 ft.) above sea level. It was sad to see so much destruction. Tegucigalpa, a manufacturing city of almost 300,000 people, is situated in the center of an earlier silver mining region.

Tegucigalpa, capital of Honduras, lies near the south-central area that narrows almost finger-like between El Salvador to the west and Nicaragua to the east, about 60 miles from the Pacific. Imagine standing body to body, in the heat, on one of the city's bridges!

Another home in Valle De Angels. As is typical, constructed with an adobe "brick" and red tile roof. This house has less than typical damage. Some people had the unnerving experience of being seated in one-room and eating when the other end of the house was torn away.

A Generation Of Children Wanders Ruins Of Honduras

Reprinted with permission from *USA Today*.

FEBRUARY 2, 1999

SAN PEDRO SULA, Honduras—Olbin and Edgardo Casares sleep on a piece of cardboard on a concrete platform behind an old building. They lie just above piles of trash, among a swarm of flies and mosquitoes.

The boys used to live with their parents in a small town in the Honduran countryside. But three months ago, Hurricane Mitch forever altered their lives.

Their house was washed away in a mudslide. Their father was killed. Their mother went to live with a relative who didn't want them.

So the brothers, 11 and 10, hitchhiked eight hours to San Pedro Sula, Honduras' second-largest city. Now they live like wild animals on the city's grimy streets.

Olbin and Edgardo are what social workers here call "Mitch kids," hundreds of children who live on the streets after the devastation brought by Hurricane Mitch, the worst natural disaster to hit Central America this century.

Some are on the streets because they have nowhere else to go. Others have been set out by impoverished parents.

Years after the mud dries, the effect of Hurricane Mitch will still be evident on a generation of impoverished children in this country.

"We have hundreds more kids on the streets now because of Mitch," says Juan Carlos Mathu of the San Pedro Committee for the Child, shelter for homeless children in this city of a half-million inhabitants. "Some of them have come here from towns hours away. They've lost their houses. They're begging, looking for food."

During the day, Olbin and Edgardo beg or shine shoes. Sometimes they slip into Burger

We have hundreds of kids on the streets now because of Mitch.

King to use the bathroom. At times, they cool off in the fountain the city's main square. They haven't changed their clothes in three months. They wear no shoes.

"Honduras was devastated in that hurricane," Anna Aguilar, as social worker, said last week at the children's shelter. "And as usual, it's the children that will pay the highest price. We're doing what we can, but it's such a huge problem."

More than 11,000 people died in the aftermath of the hurricane in Honduras and Nicaragua. Millions were left homeless.

"If it wasn't for Mitch, I'd be home now," says Olbin, scratching at mosquito bites on his leg. Asked whether his mother knows where he is, Olbin just shrugs. "I don't know where she is anymore. It's just me and my brother."

Eight-year-old Edwin Castro knows where his mother is. She's the one who sends him into the street each day for money.

"My mother tells me to come here and beg," says Edwin, a slight child with a large patch of fungus on his head. Edwin lives with his mother and sister under sheets of plastic beneath the stands of the city's soccer stadium. The stadium has been converted into a shelter for people made homeless by Mitch.

Millions of pounds of aid, mostly clothes, have been sent to Honduras. Millions of dollars have been pledged. And in the long run, the government hopes to build housing for most of the homeless.

But for the moment, about 1,600 people call the stadium home. They share 40 toilets. They sleep under plastic sheeting on thin mattresses spread about on the concrete floor of the stadium's perimeter.

This month, hundreds of homeless people living in city schools are moving into the stadium as authorities reclaim the buildings for the start of the academic year.

12 Years Working the Streets

"My mother says we'll have to rent a room after we leave the shelter, so we need money," Edwin said. "She's happy if I come home with 50 to 100 lempiras ($3.65 to $7.25). If I make less than that, she's not happy." He steals a tangerine

Thousands of people are left homeless.

from a street vendor and runs barefoot down the street.

Edwin and several other "Mitch kids" catch a bus to the city center from the shelter each day. They work the streets for 12 hours, then return to the shelter at night.

At times, though, they don't make it home. What starts as a way to make a little money, social workers say, quickly becomes a way of life.

"After a while, they don't come back anymore," says Mathu of the San Pedro Committee for Kids. "And then it's very hard to get them off the streets."

Those who stick with the shelter sleep five and six to a mattress. They roam the stadium in gangs. Many get hooked on sniffing shoe glue.

"There's nothing for these children to do in the shelters," says Blanca Estela Rodriguez, the Honduras director for Children International, a Kansas City-based relief agency working with impoverished children around the world.

"They don't have any alternatives."

Social workers from Children International work in the shelters, trying to help the children.

People cannot live like this for very long," Rodriguez says, "If the government doesn't do something soon, the problem will just get worse."

Disease Rampant

Disease is a constant menace for all the children, those in the shelters and those living in makeshift shacks near the river where their homes once stood.

Mosquitoes bred in the stagnant water carry malaria and dengue fever. The dirty water, where people bathe and children play, spreads hepatitis. Rats carry leptospirosis, a deadly disease that causes liver and kidney failure and ultimately death.

"We've had respiratory problems, diarrhea, malaria, all kinds of problems," says Fabricio Rodezno, a Honduran doctor working with Children International.

"With all the rain we've had and the overcrowding in the shelters, one mosquito can infect dozens of people."

In Las Brisas, a riverbank suburb of San Pedro Sula, Maria Angela Sanchez and her four

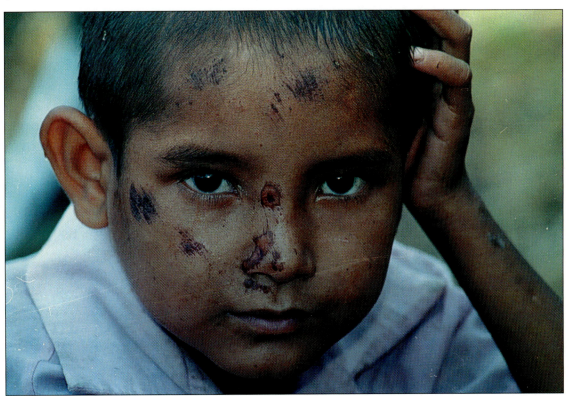

Diseases could quickly take hold. Eye infections, diarrhea and skin rashes are already widespread.

children, ages 3 months to 5 years, wait to see one of the volunteer doctors who make the rounds of the poor.

"All of my children are sick," Sanchez says. "The 5-year-old has stomach pains, the 3-year-old has a fever and diarrhea, the 1 1/2-year-old has a bad cough and diarrhea, and the baby has a cough and a fever."

The Kids Go On

It's not difficult to understand why. People defecate in alleys; dogs rummage in the piles of muck. And everyone bathes in the dirty river.

But somehow life goes on. And so do the children.

One of the kids in the clinic is 13-year-old Jose Rene Montufar. He works 12 hours a day in a carpenter's shop for 200 lempiras a week ($14.50). Jose came to the clinic complaining of a bad sore throat and a high fever.

After examining Jose, the nurse hands him a packet of tablets and explains what to take and when. "This child should go to bed now," says the nurse, Xiomara Moradel. "He's got a high fever, he's anemic and quite ill."

Asked where he would go after the examining is over, Jose shrugs, "I'm going back to work. We need the money."

More people being rescued.

A family using a horse for transportation.

Three That Mitch Spared

Printed with permission from *Honduras This Week*.

FEBRUARY 13, 1999

TEGUCIGALPA—They're smiling now. Last October, when the placid Choluteca River turned into a raging torrent, surging over its banks, pulverizing dikes and washing away adobe shanties and corrugated cardboard huts in its path, Miguel, Rafael and Edgar, street-smart but not immortal, faced nature's fury with a mixture of fascination and dread. They also took stock of life's utter fragility in ways children should never know.

If the street is a cruel master, the lessons in survival it teaches homeless minors are not soon forgotten. Living by their wits since they were less than half their present age, Miguel, 12, Rafael, 16 and Edgar, also 16, saw the waters rise, "like soup boiling over in a kettle," and felt the ground grumble underfoot "like a stampeding herd of buffalos."

It is difficult for kids who have faced the horror of street life to emote strongly about any tragedy, even a cataclysm such as Mitch.

Written off by two older brothers, Rafael, whose mother died and who has "no place to go," nodded in quiet acquiescence.

At first, the boys slept outdoors, seeking higher ground huddling together against the walls of collapsed buildings. Every morning, they rifled through garbage bins for food. During the day they begged or pilfered trinkets from unwary vendors and sold them in the peatonal. Later, they sought refuge under the shantytown that stretches across the river between two bridges on the Comayaguela side of town There they scavenged for anything they could salvage and sell: an iron bed frame; tires; a bicycle; a pair of rubber boots; a clock.

It is difficult for kids who have faced the horror of street life to emote strongly about any tragedy, even a cataclysm such as Mitch.

The remains of the foundations pictured in the foreground are still more of the destruction caused by the flooded Choluteca River in Comayaguela.

There was a village in this picture. The path of devastation from the mudslide went through this area. Notice the size of boulders and logs that were moved by the force of the mudslide.

Heart to Heart Helps North Coast Community

Printed with permission from *Honduras This Week*.

FEBRUARY 20, 1999

SANTA ROSA DE AGUAN–Along the North Coast of Honduras are numerous Garifuna communities with a combined population of more than 100,000. Descendants of black slaves and Caribbean Indians, this ethnic group exists mainly at a subsistence level on the bounty of nature: coconut palms furnish coconuts, manioc provides cassava, and the rivers and ocean supply fish.

In the bottom tier of Honduran society, this group was also one of the hardest hit by Hurricane Mitch. Santa Rosa de Agaun, a village near the municipality of Trujillo, suffered the most. Flooding from torrential rains swept the fresh water fish into the sea along with people, cattle, pigs and chickens. They either drowned or died from the salt. Fishing in the river is poor now, many of the *cayucos* (dug-out canoes) were swept to sea along with fishing nets. The tragedies of those losses compound other losses.

When Dr. Seven Foster, from Heart to Heart, a relief mission based in Dalton, Georgia was asked when school would start again, no one could answer. The teacher, her husband and her four sons had all been swept out to sea. A week later, the teacher was picked up by a British warship, clinging to a floating log. None of her family were found. Of all the people swept out to sea in Santa Rosa de Aguan, she is the sole survivor.

When several parts of the kindergarten floor collapsed as team members of Heart to Heart were cleaning the building, they realized they had to move. The group relocated and set up a health clinic in the community recreation center. For eight days they treated respiratory infections, pneumonia, and asthma, pulled teeth, and dressed the many puncture wounds caused by nails and other flying debris during the storm.

A teacher, her husband and her four sons had all been swept out to sea. A week later the teacher was picked up by a British warship, as she was found clinging to a floating log. None of her family were found. Of all the people swept out to sea, she is the sole survivor.

The devastation was most thorough along the Choluteca River in the capital city of Tegucigalpa. Sparing neither buildings nor bridges, many who knew the city well, now hardly recognized the changed landscape. These photos, dated November 13, 1998 give evidence of the force created by the water of Mitch. D.S.H.

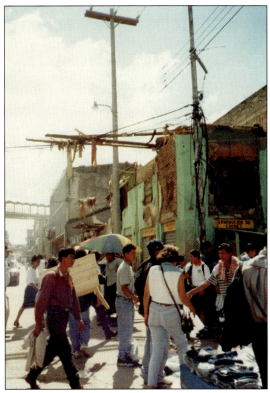

In the heart of Comayaguela you can see how high the water was by the debris on the wires. This city dates back into the 16th Century. There is no record of the city ever experiencing such devastation as from Mitch. It's no wonder the Hondurans nicknamed this hurricane "witch" instead of Mitch.

Charlotte and Kathleen in Valle De Angels (Valley of Angels) in mid-December about six weeks after Mitch hit, leaving a troubled path.

Rebuilding Will Be An Awesome Job

News used with permission from different sources.

MARCH 4, 1999

TEGUCIGALPA, Honduras–The Choluteca River reeks of sewage in the early morning, but the dozen men digging up its banks don't seem to mind. They burrow into the mounds of sand, soil and debris left by Hurricane Mitch's floodwaters, looking for buried treasure.

A salvageable tire would be great. A car would be like a gold mine – it could be stripped and its parts sold. Ramon Miralda digs down five feet and tosses out a rubber boot. Not much use, he says, unless he finds its pair.

The men on the river bank are doing the same thing that leaders across Central America are doing, four months after Hurricane Mitch devastated their region. They are looking deep into the ruins for some kind of treasure.

While the storm killed thousands and knocked down houses, bridges and crops, it also created opportunities.

Millions of dollars in aid have flowed into the region and much of its foreign debt – Honduras owes $4.3 billion, Nicaragua $6 billion – could be forgiven. Airports are buzzing with aid workers, doctors and engineers arriving from around the world to help rebuild.

Hondurans, for one, see a chance to shake off their "banana republic" image and build a richer, stronger country out of the muck and destruction. Few Hondurans would be satisfied to rebuild what they had before the storm – one of the poorest nations in the hemisphere.

"The people don't want what they had before Mitch. The people want things better than before. And they want it now," said Moises Starkman, Honduras' minister for international cooperation.

One of those opportunities for change

Rescuers dig through tons of mud, debris and decomposing bodies.

comes Monday when President Clinton arrives for a four-day tour of Central America to see the damage and discuss solutions.

Central America is looking for more from the United States than the $956 million in emergency aid Clinton has proposed. Leaders want Washington to lower trade barriers and give Central American businesses access to U.S. consumers similar to what Mexicans have under the North American Free Trade Agreement.

Before Mitch, Honduras or Nicaragua would have had little hope of boosting their trade status. Now they may have a chance. Clinton has endorsed the concept of freer trade with Central America, and there's also support in the U.S. Congress.

"To me, the question is: Are we going to essentially ignore the economic needs of some of our nearest neighbors who have just suffered a crippling blow?" said Sen. Bob Graham, D-Fla., who recently toured the region.

Even with international help and the possible easing of trade barriers, rebuilding will be an awesome job.

Thousands of people remain without housing. Broken sewage lines pose health threats, and aid agencies warn of a food crisis this spring. Heavy rains could set off more flooding and landslides. Honduras' agricultural industry – the main source of foreign earnings – is in ruin.

Also, the farms of these people were completely annihilated. Farms along the Coco River flood plain are in a prime location because the river provides plenty of soil nutrients. Combined with fallow methods of farming, the indigenous people have some of the most productive land in Nicaragua. Bananas, rice, beans, corn, coconuts, and plantains are cultivated in abundance in this region. However, the flooding and landslides caused by the passing of Hurricane Mitch tore up all of the farmland. Now, the people along the Coco River are entirely dependent on food from emergency assistance programs.

Making matters worse, the indigenous people are having trouble being reached by emergency relief assistance efforts because of their geographic isolation. For land deliveries, the emergency relief crews are forced to travel

Hurricane Mitch is considered one of the worst natural disasters ever occurring in the Western Hemisphere.

through incredibly rough terrain and have to meet members of the indigenous communities at halfway points. These halfway points are usually along the course of a river to which the people can take a canoe or boat.

Also, the shortage of helicopters in the country has limited the amount of emergency airlifts. As of Tuesday, November 10, only two airlifts had been made to communities along the Coco River. These deliveries consisted of food, medical supplies, clothes, and fresh water.

Emergency Relief Needed

Much of this relief assistance is being arranged by non-governmental organizations that have close ties to the indigenous populations in the Bosawas Reserve. Besides Alistar-Nicaragua, the Nature Conservancy and GZT (a German technical assistance agency) have been working feverishly to provide any assistance possible.

The British military have also been able to provide help from one of its warships sailing off the Atlantic Coast. Despite all this, many people along the Coco River have gone days without any food or water whatsoever.

Though immediate rescue and relief is of the utmost importance, problems of epidemiological crises are imminent. It is likely that there will be an outbreak of cholera, already a regular problem for the people living near the Coco. Water from the river, with its load of human and animal waste, has contaminated local wells, and in most cases, is the only water supply currently available.

Government agencies have issued numerous warnings about a cholera epidemic and the NGOs have made cholera prevention a number one priority. The recommendation is to boil the water and add a few drops of bleach to each gallon, letting it sit for ten minutes before drinking.

Nevertheless, for the indigenous people, possible epidemics are problems too far in the future to concern themselves with. "They are still in shock...they are living day to day, and aren't thinking about these things," said Murrar.

Murrar predicts that relief efforts will be needed for the next three to five months. After

The farms of these people were completely annihilated. Farms along the Coco River flood plain are in a prime location because the river provides plenty of soil nutrients.

However, flooding and landslides caused by the passing of Hurricane Mitch tore up all of the farmland.

For land deliveries, the emergency relief crews are forced to travel through incredibly rough terrain and have to meet members of indigenous communities at halfway points.

that, there will most likely be a reconstruction period lasting several years. This will consist of rebuilding houses, schools, and churches, and the reorganization of farms. In terms of development, it is estimated that these communities have been set back almost ten years.

Close to Nature

Fortunately, the indigenous people's long history of living and farming along the river has allowed them to gain extensive knowledge of how the river and the land works. "With the passing of each hurricane, the river always gets flooded," Murrar stated. "They know how to handle these natural disasters because they are very close to nature."

Despite the degree of devastation caused by Hurricane, there is great confidence here that the indigenous people along the Coco River will overcome this great disaster.

It will be recalled that the hurricane took place at the end of October. The first food relief did not reach the Mosquitia until Dec. 5, when 47 tons arrived. The problem then became a matter of getting the food distributed to 49 communities spread out along a 250 mile stretch of the Rio Patuca.

Of course, the international aid distributed by the World Food Program helped greatly, but the cupboard is now bare in many places, he said. There is however, no lack of food, as the PMA has accumulated many tons which are now sitting in the harbor at Puerto Costes.

Benitez said the problem has been in getting it shipped to the Mosquitia. For two months, he added, tribal leaders from the region have petitioned the military as well as other governmental agencies for a boat, but have received nothing.

U.S. forces alone saved 650 people huddling on rooftops or clinging to trees. Honduran forces rescued thousands more.

Many of the homeless were not so blessed in finding temporary shelter, since the schools and other public buildings quickly filled to overflowing. Since the four-lane highway, going from San Pedro Sula, east, through La Lima and El Progreso was the highest point in the area, the median became the site of a new "tent city." Hundreds of families erected make-shift shelters with whatever materials could be found. Sanitation was nonexistent and comfort nearly so. With rains continuing in the weeks following the storm and inadequate shelters such as these, it continued to be a miserable muddy existence for many. D.S.H.

Charlotte, Oscar and Norma Jean, top left, observing the deep cut and dangling lines in a village close to the Seventh Day Adventist Hospital which was spared. Charlotte found the hospital personnel to be gracious and most helpful. Crisis should bring forth our best and challenge us to Christ's likeness. It is essential to remember, all events that occurred are ultimately under God's control and our awareness of them valuable for our growth.

Notice the outhouse (toilet) left standing on the left…on the very edge of the mudslide. Can we imagine the gratitude of the recipients of the 5-gallon buckets and packages prepared and sent by individuals in Charlotte's home community? Beans, rice, corn, medical and school supplies, clothing were among the items being sent.

Global Project to Help Farmers Hurt by Hurricane Mitch

Printed with permission from *Honduras This Week*.

Grant Scobie, director general of the International Center for Tropical Agriculture (CIAT) in Colombia, another of the groups supporting the project in Central America, said that "without rapid action to restore food production, Nicaragua and Honduras will face not only serious nutrition and health problems, but severe economic and social problems whose effects will be felt throughout the region. About half of the work force in these countries is employed in the agricultural sector."

He added that unless the agricultural sectors are quickly revived, thousands of farmers and their families will migrate to urban areas and nearby countries. Seeds of Hope, he said, is "critical to sustainably re-establishing the food production of small farmers in Honduras and Nicaragua."

"Without rapid action to restore food production, Nicaragua and Honduras will face not only serious nutrition and health problems, but severe economic and social problems whose effects will be felt throughout the region. About half of the work force in these countries is employed in the agricultural sector."

Project-backers hope to encourage farmers to plant sweet potatoes alongside corn, a practice that has helped reduce soil erosion in China. That is because sweet potatoes, which grow below ground, serve to anchor loose soil. They also require little fertilizer while producing a high volume of crops per hectare. Because sweet potatoes provide an excellent source of vitamin A, the Nicaraguan government is said to strongly support their reintroduction into the country to improve nutrition.

Experts estimate that Hurricane Mitch

Many of the bridges were damaged, as the one in this picture.

destroyed up to 70 percent of the basic food crops of Honduras and Nicaragua. Nicaragua lost about 60 percent of its bean crop and 40 percent of its maize crop. In Honduras, 75 percent of the bean crop and about half of the maize crop was lost. Other Honduran subsistence crops, including potatoes and plantains, also suffered considerable damage, and many crop varieties were destroyed.

Additionally, the storm caused heavy damage to the natural resources that support agriculture. In many places, Mitch caused massive soil erosion, exposing subsoil and rocks and severely damaging the land's productive capacity. High levels of silt in rivers jeopardized water supplies for irrigation and energy generation.

Organizers said satellite technology will be used to provide "an extraordinarily detailed picture" of the worst-hit agricultural areas, and the areas which are at the risk of further degradation. Citizens of those areas will receive help in using modern agricultural techniques to improve their land management and crop yields.

"This is the only way to prevent similar catastrophic results from recurring," said CIAT's Grant Scobie. "One reason natural disasters are so devastating to developing countries is that poverty and poor land management put pressure on the land. For example, when people deforest local hillsides, they increase the risk of mudslides in heavy rains. Already, we're finding that in areas where the farms in Nicaragua and Honduras were properly managing the land before the hurricane, the damage is less severe."

A river overflowing into the streets.

Orphaned by Mitch
Children of Hope

Reprinted with permission by *Nica News*.

In the Chinandega Hospital, Norlan Javier lies on a bed cradling a pink balloon. He is one of eight children in the Chinandega department documented so far as having lost both parents as a result of the disaster. The Ministry of Family does not know how many other children like Norlan are scattered about the affected zones. They are gathering information from around the country and believe there will be more.

On Friday, October 30 at around 12:30 p.m., Norlan Javier and his two cousins were caught and swept up in the river of mud roaring down the slopes off Casita Volcano, covering what was once their home, El Porvenir. Norlan Javier and his cousins are three of 134 survivors from a village of over 600 people.

Though he has lost his parents, Norlan Javier has not been abandoned. Less than 24 hours after his arrival at the hospital, an uncle came looking for survivors. He will take care of his own son, Norlan Javier, and the other cousin.

Wanting to Care

"These children are all I have left in the world," he said. No other members of his immediate family survived, and his house and village are no more.

"Many of the children in the hospital in Chinandega are in a state of shock. They cry out at night. They ask for toys, a stuffed animal, a doll. They are looking for comfort and a way to express their feelings," said Jose Leonel Jimenez of Mifamilia's Public Relations.

In some cases, the kids do not recognize the person coming to claim them, either because the child is too young or the family member is a distant relative. In these cases the family member must have witnesses to prove that they really are related," Ramon Diaz explained.

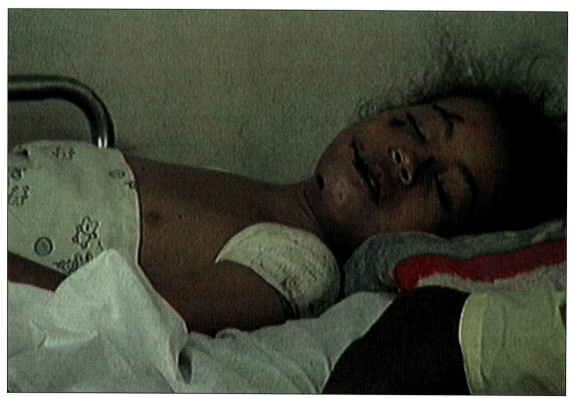

Many children in the hospital are in a state of shock. They cry out at night, and are looking for comfort.

This is one of the houses that was damaged from the mudslide in Charlotte Shank's area. Some of the people have plans to rebuild, but others have left to go live in Tegucigalpa.

Sheldon Yoder from Ohio (standing at right) was always popular with his candy bag. Many children are homeless. We invited 12 to 15 children for a children's class one evening. Imagine our surprise when over 200 children arrived!

Charlotte Shank's Story of Living Through Hurricane Mitch

Printed with permission.

I came to Honduras in August of 1998 to teach English at United Faith Bilingual School in Valle de Angeles. I was assured upon my arrival, by the founders and administrators of the school, Mike and Becky Kauffman, that Honduras was a very "safe" place to be. They told me that there are no volcanos, earthquakes or hurricanes here and that Honduras had had 25 years since it's last natural disaster. "Things like that just don't happen here," they explained

All went fairly well getting settled in to teaching and adjusting to living in a different culture. I had made some friends and was preparing for our first bi-mester exams when we heard that Mitch was coming. Nobody seemed to be worried and we continued our regular schedule with the exams. When we have exams, we have them everyday for a week and then we have half days all week.

The weather on that Monday, October 26th, was cloudy and a light drizzle was falling. Mike told me that morning that a hurricane was coming and so as soon as the children finished their exams for the day, they could go home. (That made them all quite happy!) They finished quickly and went home to wait out the storm. We told them to come back tomorrow for more exams unless the storm had hit.

Well, nothing happened the rest of that day. Mike had told me to pack a bag with a weeks supply of clothes and such so that if the storm hit, they could pick me up and take me along with them to Becky's mom's house. We went to Tegucigalpa that Monday afternoon to stock up on groceries and other items that we might run low on. It was all rather exciting and kind of reminded me of the States when were expecting a big snowstorm.

Tuesday morning dawned, and it was exactly the same as Monday. Only a bit of drizzle and a lot of clouds and fog. The children came to school, but by

This is a view of the peaceful mountain town of Valle De Angeles, Honduras. About one month before Mitch, the small white house to far right of picture is Hamish & Rachel's house where I was when the landslide occurred. Please note that the creek that the landslide followed isn't visible because it was so small.

8:30 a.m. the government had cancelled all the classes for the whole nation. So everyone was sent home again, until further notice. The teachers were informed that there was to be a meeting in the "town hall" (I guess that is what you would call it) that they were required to attend that evening. Miss Martha came by and walked with me to the meeting. All the teachers and professors and head people of the village were there. We discussed plans for food collection to help areas that would undoubtable be hit hard, emergency housing for this village and emergency feeding plans for people who might run out of food. They meeting moved along rather swiftly and the town seemed fairly well prepared for the storm. We didn't expect to be hit hard here in the mountains, but were preparing just in case. Toward the end of the meeting some police came in and asked for the mayor and some of the other people to come and help them with some evacuations. (I forgot to mention that it had started raining very hard by 11 a.m. and never seemed to let up. We had also had a lot of rain in the preceding week.) There were some mountain homes that were starting to collapse but the people didn't want to leave them and come to a safer building in the village. These houses were made of adobe bricks, which are very economical for the poor to use in construction. However, with all the rain, the water couldn't drain from the land and the bricks were soaking it up, making the walls of the homes very unstable. They would start to bulge from the weight of the roof, then eventually collapse. The people were hesitant to leave all their things that they had worked all their lives for and go to live in the village. The police had to resort to force in a few cases. There were about 20 - 30 families evacuated that night. It then began to sink in that we may have some serious problems due to this storm.

Tuesday, I also began to be concerned for my friends who lived and worked next door to me in the orphanage. Hamish, Rachel and baby Seth were on vacation in the Bay Islands with Hamish's parents, who were visiting them from England. I was praying for their safety as I had heard that Mitch was already battering the Bay Island area.

Wednesday, the rain continued to pour, as it had all night long. At one point in the day, Mike and Becky came and took me to Becky's mom's house. After being there for half an hour and seeing all the confusion and such that goes along with having 17 people confined in one house, I chose to come back to the village when Mike was returning to get something, and wait out the storm in my quiet, little apartment in the school. I figured at least I would have time to plan out my lessons for the next bi-mester and I did have my neighbors to talk to if I got lonely. I was really hoping that Rachel and Hamish could return before the storm hit too hard. I remember praying for them frequently that day, and late that evening they came straggling in. They had managed to get the last boat off the Islands to La Ceiba and to get the last bus from La Ceiba to Tegucigalpa, where they caught a bus to Valle de Angeles. God had protected them and provided for their safe return. (Their return trip wasn't without adventure, but they were kept safe.)

That night the rain really began. I thought it had rained hard before, but that was nothing compared to this. But we didn't have any wind at all, which seemed very strange as that is one of the main characteristics of a hurricane. We still had electricity, so we gathered in one of the neighbor's houses to watch the news. We learned that a storm was also coming into Honduras from the Pacific Ocean and that the two storms had locked each other into position. That is why there wasn't any wind, but now we were in for even more rain.

I don't think any of us were really scared. I spent a lot of time in the orphanage helping out with the work there, since I didn't have any school. I spent a lot of time with the McDonald's (Hamish, Rachel, Seth and Hamish's parents) visiting, telling stories and generally having a good time together. Our greatest worry at the moment was running out of dry clothes to wear. It was cold and damp all the time. I had taken to wearing my long-johns under my long skirts to keep warm. There isn't any heat in the houses to knock off the chill.

I don't remember exactly when the water and electricity cut off - but I think it was sometime on Thursday or Friday. It was still raining heavily all the time so we just set out buckets to catch rain water for washing and to sterilize for drinking. We also had stocked up on candles. It was still rather fun and sort of like going to a primitive cabin for the weekend.

Just to give you an idea of the amount of rain we received in these few days, we had an empty 6 foot deep pool on the school's property. It was empty due to some very bad leaks which made it impossible to keep full. Well, by Friday, this pool was completely full and overflowing. If it had been warm we would have gone swimming.

On Friday, Hamish's parents were supposed to leave for England again. Needless-to-say, their flight was cancelled and their "vacation" extended. They weren't too upset about it and actually seemed to be enjoying the experience to a certain extent.

Around this time there were no more candles or food to buy in the village. We realized that people were beginning to get a bit scared because they didn't have large quantities of food stored up in their houses. People often buy their food from day to day, because many do not have refrigerators or space to store food.

Friday, when I was out walking during a brief break in the rain, I had three people approach me and ask for money in 20 minutes time. That was the first time I had any real fear. I remembered reading that at times, when natural disasters occur in foreign countries, the people there tend to think that since you are from the States, you have lots of extra money, food, clothes and such laying around to give to them. Sometimes when people become desperate, they can be violent toward North Americans. I returned to my apartment and prayed for protection from such people. I was never asked for money again. This was another answer to my prayer.

That evening after a candlelight supper, several of us got together to sing and praise the God we share. We had a good time of worship and prayer. We all knew that whatever happened we were all in the hands of God and He was in control of the situation.

Friday night I didn't sleep very well. There is a small creek about 300 yards or so from my house. This had turned into a small, but raging and constantly rising river. All night I could hear the rocks grinding and clinking together as they were washed down stream with the water. It wasn't a pleasant sound.

I wasn't scared because the road to the creek really slopes down from my house and I knew it would flood in the other direction first. It was just an unfamiliar noise that disturbs your sleep.

Saturday morning we could hear the river much clearer and louder. It still continued to rain. At one point in the morning several of us took our cameras and went to several places where a road would cross

We didn't expect to be hit hard here in the mountains.

the river. All the bridges were washed away already, except one. We didn't walk up to that one because it had started raining harder again. If we had, we might have realized some of the danger we were in. A lot of trees that had fallen down had washed up against that bridge and had formed a big dam that was holding lots of water, mud, rocks and more trees. This was located just up the mountain a bit from the village. There was some debate in the village as to what direction this flood of water would go if it let loose. It could go directly down the road that led straight through the village or it could follow the path of the creek which sort of skirted the village, but had lots of houses there too. Farther up the mountain, there are lots of vacant mines. Some of the village officials walked up there to inspect them on Friday or Saturday. They were concerned because the mines were completely filled with water and the ground was saturated. However, my friends and I knew nothing about this until sometime later that morning. Some police came by and said that there was a restaurant that we could evacuate to if we felt we needed to. The persons in charge of the orphanage decided that since we were about as high as the restaurant, we would just keep the children (about 100 of them) and staff on site. Hamish, Rachel, Hamish's parents and I passed the rest of the morning drinking hot coffee and talking in Hamish's living room. Somehow the subject of landslides came up. We weren't too worried, but we all knew that it was a remote possibility. I had just watched a program on TV at Mike's house about two weeks before this, on landslides. In the back of my mind I kept thinking that there was actually a chance of this happening here. We had the mountains and definitely had had sufficient rain for such an occurrence. But, we all kept saying that we knew we were in God's hands and didn't worry about what might be.

Around 1 p.m., Hamish left the house to go and check on some other friends and see if he could help them with anything. Shortly after that we realized we could hear the river even louder and thought it might be closer. When we looked out the window of Hamish's house we could now see the river. Before, there had been too much vegetation around so it had kept it hidden. The river was located about 100 yards down a somewhat steep hill from the house. We were a bit more concerned at this point, but it was still a good ways away. Around 2:15 or so, Rachel decided to go and have a look around the orphanage to make sure things were running smoothly. That left Hamish's parents and me in the house with Seth. I was trying to put Seth to sleep and the others were basically waiting around for a break in the rain so we could go out and stretch our legs some.

That was when everything broke loose. Seth had just gone to sleep and I was laying him down on the

Piles of mud, rocks and trees left by the mudslide.

bed, when I heard a horrible, horrible sound. I can't really describe what it is like. The ground began to tremble and I knew at once that there was a landslide coming. About the same time I heard Hamish's dad screaming to grab the baby and run. We didn't take time to find jackets, shoes or anything. I just grabbed Seth and ran with Hamish's mom from the house. When I got outside I looked to the right where the noise was coming from. There, about 20 to 30 yards from me, was a 50 foot high 100 foot wide wall of mud, water, rocks, trees, houses and other things hurling straight toward me at around 40 miles an hour. (I was told later that that is about how fast it traveled.) I can't describe my exact feelings in that moment. I remember running as fast as I could, but all the while knowing it was useless. I could hear Rachel screaming, "MY BABY!! MY BABY!!" as she ran toward the house. She said later that it looked as if we would all be swallowed up by the landslide in another second.

I will never forget the protection of the Lord on that day. Very suddenly the whole slide turned and spread out into the field below the orphanage. It had missed the house and us by about 45 feet. I remember feeling completely numb for the first 15 to 20 minutes after this. I had somehow returned to the house for my camera and taken some pictures, but I don't have a clear memory of doing this. The incredible disbelief set in. None of us could actually realize what had just happened. In the matter of minutes, 40 or more homes were destroyed, I don't know the actual number, but have counted the remains of 38 homes and I know that many more have completely disappeared leaving no trace at all. One of the mines way up the mountain had given away and as it rushed down, it burst many more open and took them along. When this hit the bridge where the dam already was, it was just too much. It all gave away. Some headed down the road toward the village, but most of it went with the river. The bit that went down the road soon lost it's power and didn't do a lot of damage there in comparison to the rest which went with the river.

Those of us in the orphanage held a prayer meeting for protection and for those people who lost all they had in this disaster. The McDonald's all moved into my house then, since none of us felt very secure in their house. And we were uncertain about the possibilities that this could happen again. Amazingly, only one person died in this landslide.

A 50 foot high, 100 foot wide wall of mud, water, rocks, trees, houses and other things came hurtling straight toward me at around 40 miles an hour.

Most of the homes that were affected had been previously evacuated.

The men that worked in the orphanage worked day and night. During the day, they along with the boys, ages 8 and up, gathered and chopped firewood for the cooks to use to make the food, picking or guarding the fields of maize, (looting was becoming a problem), carrying water from the storm drains in the village to use for bathing, washing laundry and cleaning, and fixing leaks in the buildings. At night, they took turns guarding the orphanage. The people of the village knew that there was lots of food, clothes and medicine in the orphanage and even though we were sharing them with the village, there was still the threat of a break in. People were getting more and more restless as time when on and we still didn't have any running water or electricity.

By Sunday the rain had slowed down drastically. Now we only had an occasional downpour with long periods of drizzle between. Sometime on Sunday, the sun came out for a few minutes and there was a beautiful double rainbow directly over the area destroyed in the landslide.

The village quickly organized and started to reconstruct the bridges that had been lost. We were amazed at how fast all this happened and it was done by the village people and not the foreigners living here. It was quite commendable. All able-bodied men were required to give their time and labor for this effort, except the ones working in the orphanage. (They already had their hands full). Helicopters started flying in supplies 6 to 10 times a day. At first, the orphanage children would run in terror when the chopper would circle by before landing, but soon they would be out waving at them.

On Monday or Tuesday, Hamish's parents were able to catch a free ride in one of these helicopters to the airport. There they were eventually able to catch a flight back to England. They were a great help while they were here, but we were glad that they were able to return home again.

Rachel and I busied ourselves in the mornings with all the 3-to 7-year-olds. We had some class time, reading stories, coloring, and playing games with them. It kept them from making trouble for the other staff, so they could complete their work. The children were good for the most part, but we had to watch that they didn't go down toward the river or play in water that could be contaminated. Disease was our next big concern, so we began teaching the

The mudslide spread out in the field below the orphanage.

children what things to avoid and making them wash in water containing disinfectant frequently.

With us having partial sunny days and only an occasional downpour the level of the river began to go down. It didn't rumble so much anymore and things were beginning to feel a bit more settled. Then the first people that walked from Tegucigalpa to Valle de Angeles arrived. They told us about the 22 places in 11 miles that the road would need to be repaired. There were several huge sections that simply were not there any more. Landslides had taken them away. There were many other areas where bits of the mountain had slid down on the road and would have to be cleared before vehicles could pass. They really didn't think that the road could be salvaged at all. This created new feelings of desperation. People began to say that we would we stuck here in Valle and starve because no food could be brought in by land. And they didn't think that sufficient supplies could be flown in by the helicopters. The town set a curfew from 9 p.m. to 5 a.m. to help keep the looting down and to try to keep more peace in the village. Anybody in the street during those hours would be arrested and kept in jail for a few days. The village also started to focus very strongly on getting the water and electricity going again.

On November 4th, my father's birthday, the phone worked for about 2 hours and I was able to contact my family for the first time. That was the first time I really cried since everything had happened. I knew that they had probably been worried about me, but I didn't realize to what extent they were worried. They had heard that there were landslides near Tegucigalpa and had seen lots of the destruction on the news. I think they knew more about what was and had happened in Honduras than we did. We had no access to the news since sometime on Friday before the landslide. It was a short phone call, but one filled with lots of relief and praise for the lives that were spared. A few days later, we had running water again and then two days after that we had electricity. This helped greatly in calming everyone down.

Some local construction workers went to look at the road to Tegucigalpa and discovered that it was somewhat repairable and set to work on it. By the end of the week you could go to Tegucigalpa and back by hitching rides in trucks and such for short sections and walking around the bad sections. Then it wasn't long until they had it repaired enough that

The village quickly organized and started to reconstruct the bridges.

you could drive the whole way there. (I know that in the States they would NEVER have let people drive on a road like that, but here it is a different story). Temporary bridges were built all around the village where the landslide had gone. However, the second night after they were finished it really rained hard again. We don't know for sure, but some think that another mine gave away, because the river was again very loud in the night and in the morning all the new bridges were gone again. It is really hard to know if this happened just because of the heavy rain or if it really was another slide. People were very upset and sometimes you just didn't know what to believe.

For a long time after the slide, I had trouble sleeping at night and would often have nightmares about the slide, or would feel very apprehensive when it would start to rain. November is the start of the dry season here, but it still rained frequently, which was extremely unusual. I never felt like I wanted to go home. Even though I wasn't sure exactly what I was supposed to be doing, I knew that God had me in Honduras at this time for a specific reason. Even though I may not understand why, I had peace about being here.

School was able to start again by November 18th. We spent the first few days working with the emotions of the children. It was important that they could express their feelings and work through them. From there, things have continued to improve. The road to Tegucigalpa would still give a good fright to anyone who wasn't used to it. But basic everyday life has settled back down. I was concerned that my sisters, who had planned to visit me at Christmas, wouldn't be able to make it. But, thanks to God, they could come and we had a great time together.

There were around 300 families that lost their homes here in Valle and the surrounding mountains. Many of these were because they were made of adobe. Two families in the school lost their homes and businesses, but thankfully, not their lives. There still are needs for the homeless, but the village has pulled together and helped them as much as possible. Sometimes now, I need to walk down the road to the landslide to remind myself of the events during those few weeks. I never want to forget all the ways God blessed us during that time. Many times it just seems like something that would have happened in someone else's life and not mine. However, I am sure that God has some plans for my life yet or I would have perished in that slide on October 31, 1998.

Huge sections of the road is missing.

 This 11 to 12-year-old boy said he had lived in this house, now in ruins. It is sad to think about the effects and permanent impact the storm has had on these young lives. There are many such children. We did not visit the worst areas, they are closed off and with the terrible stench we could not have handled it anyway. Even as spectators our lives were permanently impacted by the vast devastation.

 In the background is the house where Charlotte was October 31st when Mitch brought down the mudslide that providentially circled her house by perhaps 30 yards, sparing her and those with her, from the 40 foot high mud mass laced with furniture and other debris. What a reminder that God is indeed in control of our lives.

We saw these houses in the city of Comagaguela which lies across the river from Tegucigalpa. They were filled with mud. My 17-year-old sister, Norma Jean, certainly disliked seeing such a terrible mess and found it hard to believe that rain could cause so much ruin. The combination of a swollen river and mudslides from the mountains certainly created havoc.

This is an enlargement of the structure shown near the river. The day our bus stopped in Tegucigalpa was very hot and Charlotte's friend had put his hat on her for protection. During the stop a man snatched the hat from her head and ran away. Perhaps the brand name – which was Adidas – made it especially desirable.

Rebuilding Hope in the Wake of Hurricane Mitch

Printed with permission from *Peacework*.

The statistics begin to shift a bit, some weeks after Hurricane Mitch devastated parts of Honduras and its neighboring countries. As rescue missions continue and the debris of this 'Category Five' hurricane is cleared, Honduras, a small country approximately the size of Tennessee, presents an alarming dossier of destruction—7,079 confirmed deaths and 9,014 missing, with the expectation that the number of confirmed deaths will increase. Family and relatives of those who have not appeared conduct journeys to the affected areas throughout the country and conduct radio searches for their loved ones. The search is not easy—it is estimated that 20% of the Honduran population had to flee their homes initially during the flooding, with at least 80,000 homes now completely lost and hundreds of thousands of other damaged. Entire communities of people live in makeshift shelters in schools, churches, and warehouses, with relatives or friends, or simply in the rubble.

Honduras is a small country, approximately the size of Tennessee.

Of course, numbers are only partial representations of the human condition. For those of us who live and work in Honduras, the impact of Mitch is felt not only because of its magnitude, but with each face that forms part of the statistics: Angela who drowned just outside Tegucigalpa

Children and their mothers appear to be bored with little to do in this scene at "Dios Con Nosotros" Baptist Church in Puerto Cortez, a northern coastal town in Honduras. The two or three hundred homeless victims of Mitch staying at "Dios Con Nosotros" and at Franklin D. Roosevelt School, a block away, were among the more privileged as far being able to use temporary shelters. While many slept on cardboard and whatever else was available, at least these had concrete floors and a good roof. The population here was mostly women and children, since many of the men were out trying to get back to their homes and villages.

"Dios Con Nosotros" also operated a clinic. C.A.M. helped to provide food such as rice and beans to feed the refugees and provided some medical supplies for the clinic. D.S.H.

Here there was once a village. Another village was destroyed just northwest of this one.

The creek bed that led back to the volcano was dry. You can see that it was made much wider and deeper.

This was as far back as we could drive. This is where the mud began to gouge into a dry creek bed. It follows the creek bed to the ocean.

Taken from the Pan American Highway. We are about 10–12 miles from the mountain at this point.

A Story
by Jeremiah Martin

Printed with permission.

The following stories are from the town of Ceibita, a relatively small town approximately 10 kil. from the city of Sava. The Aguan River, wide and muddy, flows through this large fertile valley. The heart of the economy is quite visibly the extensive banana plantations that line both sides of the river. Of course, the beating these plantations have received from "Mitch" are tremendous, actually the whole valley, from Sava all the way to the north coast is one of the hardest hit areas in Honduras.

Rene Sinclair tells how he sent his wife and eight children to Sava to pass the storm. "I stayed back to watch the house," he says. "I was awakened that night by the water in my bed. In a flash, I got up and began to carry the things I could, out of my house into by sisters house, that was a little higher. I then went to another house, across the road to pass the night. Well, there were already some others in that house, looking for safety, because it was situated on a higher bank. About midnight the water reached a threatening height, even on the bank, so we all decided to bail out. Just in time! As we left, the house also decided to call it quits, and it was gone. Where do we go from here? Our sights were set on a well built block house on this same bank. Gratefully, we arrived to the only house in town that was not under water. You can well image how many people were there, by morning the number had grown to 500! Everyone shared the little or much we had. The small food store owners shared the food they had secured.

Other residents of the town found refuge in the nearby banana plantations packing house. "We got hungry in there," related Alfredo Chirindo. A calf came struggling by, so we jumped in the water and caught our meal. The

"I was awakened that night by water in my bed."

111

next day we managed to catch three pigs. The big scare of the whole ordeal was the night we felt the building shake, everyone thought this was it. What did we find at daybreak? A sea container resting against the stilts of the building! On the third day a few of us swam to our houses and brought back some good oranges. This same day we received a few sacks of food from the first helicopter drop-off.

Fortunately, no lives were lost from this town, but many were not as fortunate upstream, and were left to decay alongside of cows, horses, pigs, etc. The pastor of the town's pentecostal church seems to have led the town in clean-up. I told the men to start very early in the morning because by 9:00 a.m. we were not able to take the smell any longer.

A local television station, we were told, carried the story of a daring young boy, I don't know from what town, who was riding on trunks of trees, floating with the current. All at once he spotted a briefcase floating down the current, retrieving it and to his surprise, found the wish of practically every poor boy in Honduras. Yes, you guessed it, money.

Water rushing at high speed taking with it whatever was in its path.

A man being rescued by cables, where part of a bridge had collapsed.

Relief Work in Honduras

Printed with permission from *Jacob Bear*.

Greetings to all again in the name of Him who was "pleased as man with men to dwell, Jesus our Immanuel."

On November 3, I arrived at Hummingbird for what I thought was to be a two-week visit. My trip had been delayed for one week because of Hurricane Mitch's presence in the Caribbean; flights into Belize City were being cancelled. I had watched the progress of the storm very carefully during that week. It was good, after arriving in Belize, to learn of hurricane relief work beginning in Honduras. I was encouraged to stay another two weeks to help with that work, I was grateful for the privilege, and am glad that I stayed. There were some problems that prevented our going when we first planned, but the second week things were in order, and we began our trip.

Our group from central Belize left Hummingbird on Sunday, November 22, and went to David Stutzman's at Punta Gorda. There were to be 12 of us in this first group going over to do actual relief work. Those from Hummingbird were Eugene Hursh, Michael Hofer and I. From the Beachy Church at Isabella Bank; David Glick, and Erwin, a native Honduran who is living in Belize and is under instruction at that church; from the Cayo side; Paul Kauffman and Aaron, 18 or 19 years old and attending church at Cayo; two Shipyard Mennonite men; Felipe and his nephew whose name I can't remember; a Spanish Lookout man, Menno, from Punta Gorda; David Stutzman and Clifford Schrock.

On Monday the sea was too rough for our boat trip, so we helped with last-minute preparations for the trip, and in the afternoon got to help with the construction of a house in Blue Creek. Finally on Tuesday morning, Paco, the boat owner, and his sailor thought it was safe to go to Honduras. The boat was small–24 ft. long and 5 ft. wide–loaded with 14 men and all our belongings. We crashed through eight-foot seas for four hours, and it was a very rough crossing. We arrived at Puerto Cortez on the north side of Honduras, and two of our group remained there to help with the receiving and handling of relief goods being shipped to that military port. The rest of us bused to San Pedro Sula and from there to the town of El Progreso.

In El Progreso, an empty hardware store had been rented for warehouse storage and housing for the relief workers. The old showroom floor is now being used for storage for stacks of sacked corn, beans and rice. Above the showroom is a big balcony that served as an excellent dormitory. A turn to the right and another flight of stairs, and you were in the house built on top of the hardware store. There were three Spanish Lookout couples there when we arrived, and they had supper ready for us.

After a good night's sleep, we had breakfast and were ready to go. But since we were the very first work group there for cleanup and rebuilding, there was no work yet lined up for us. So while David Stutzman and the Spanish Lookout man in charge planned and scheduled our week, the rest of us got busy re-sacking corn, rice, and beans into 5-lb. sacks for distribution. In the afternoon I was asked to go to a village two miles away to talk to the president of the village. I asked if we could go in and help them clean up their village and make it more livable. He said, "Yes, they would be grateful for our help to clean up their community.

Virtually the whole town had been under water during the hurricane flooding, except for the schoolhouse, which was on a mound about 10 feet above the village level. About 105 families had lived in this village of Guatalupe, and some of them had left for higher ground as the river water rose. About 70 families decided to stay. However, about 9 o'clock one night the water came over the road, which was really a dike, and began flooding the town. One man told me that everyone was wading water, waist deep, to get to the schoolhouse. The water continued rising until it was 5 /2 feet deep in the school building, so they all climbed up into the rafters of the schoolhouse. Seventy families were in the top of that schoolhouse for 2 1/2 days without food or water. During our cleanup I looked at the school ceiling and saw big holes in the plaster. I asked what had made those, and they said, "That is where some of our wives and children fell off the rafters and broke through the plaster, falling into the water below. Then we would fish them and haul them back up to safety!" One man told me that all that the children and babies did for two days was cry! But no lives in the village were lost.

One man that was in the school for those 2 1/2 days told me this. He said, "We had money in our pockets but there was nowhere to buy anything to eat. All we could do was rely on God and trust Him to see us through."

Also that 70 families were in the attic of this schoolhouse was amazing!

The schoolhouse was perhaps 100 ft. long and 30 ft. wide and the peak running longwise with the building was only 3-4 feet high in the center. It is amazing that these people survived the flood.

Another man told me of an owner of a motor boat that was fairly reliable. As soon as the water in the Alua River began to get over flood stage this man began searching for people and rescuing the ones in trouble. The man apparently worked for about four to five days, day and night by himself rescuing people. He would make one trip after another up the river to get people. Strangely enough, many mothers who saw the water rising fast and did not know where to go with their children would take their children high up in the trees along the river and actually tie them to the branches in a way that they could not come back down. Then the mother would go back down, batten down her house and climb into the tree herself and wait for help.

This man, in the motorboat, would see many, many women and children in the treetops screaming and crying for help. But the man could see that they were safe out of reach of the water. The man also knew that there were others up the river that were in more perilous danger and so he would go on by and get the ones in more danger first. He worked long and hard until he was so tired that he could not go on. Then he would tie his boat to a tree and lie down and sleep for an hour or so then wake up and work another day and night. Who knows how many people this man saved!

At another village the people pointed to a place that was now all sand and gravel. They said that there were 180 houses there before Mitch. When the flash flood came down the river, it wiped out all the houses taking 45 families with it. (I do not know it if this was fact, but it was the story they told.)

One man from up the Alua River told us about his village and what it looked like after the flood.

There were no good wells and so potable water was not available. The people were drinking bad smelly putrid water and were getting sick. He was the president of the village and had come to El Progreso to beg for food and help. He said that a herd of cattle had ran into their village after the people had all ran for high ground and the water came up and drowned the herd of cattle. When the water went down, the bodies did not wash down the river but lay in the streets. Many were in houses having floated through windows and doorways. As I recall he said there were around 140 head of dead cattle. He said the stench was unreal, overpowering. He said the people were building fires around the village to cut down the smell. He was at a loss to know what to do for his people because no one could return to their homes even though the houses had not been washed away.

In my initial visit to the president of the village, I told him and his people that we would supply food each day to every household that supplied labor to help us clean the town. I told him we wanted everyone possible to help; old men, little boys, even women, if they wanted. Meanwhile, the other fellows of our group were buying wheelbarrows, sharpening machetes, getting shovels and cleaning the warehouse.

The next morning, November 26, we started the cleanup in the village of Guatalupe. Fifty men and boys were there the first morning, ready to be put to work. Each man got a wheelbarrow or shovel or machete, and someone wrote down what each man had. At the end of the day every person was responsible to turn in the tool he had been issued that morning. We started through the village and moved block by block. The first day we did only 2 1/2 blocks, but progress was made.

The work was dirty; we walked in four to six inches of mud constantly, and sometimes it was up to 12 inches. Out of the mud we pulled metal roofing, bedsprings, clothes, wet and muddy mattresses, sugar cane, parts of trees and lots of other stuff. The wood debris was almost all saved and cut up for cooking firewood. We sweated and heaved and pushed and slipped and almost fell. We cleaned weeds and branches out of the rafters of some houses, we cut down bushes and carried mud out of houses. We cleaned fence rows and killed tarantulas and snakes. We probably averaged 10-15 snakes a day -- poisonous ones. The debris was hauled to the street and piled there for dump trucks to pick up later.

One elderly property owner got angry at the workers in his yard and told them to get out and quit cleaning, because they were taking his firewood. I was there and I said in his hearing, "This man does not want out help," and the president directed the men elsewhere. I left the scene and continued to check on the different groups in the village. About a half hour later I returned to check on the work progress, and I found several men working shoulder to shoulder with the same old man in his yard. The yard was almost clean and it looked much better. Apparently the old man had decided he wanted help after all. Fifteen minutes later I went back into his yard again to see how soon they would be done. They were just finishing the last wheelbarrow load. The old man straightened up and looked at me. I said, "Muchas gracias." He looked at me, and said, "NO!" I thought, "Oh, no, he's still mad." Then he lowered his voice and said in Spanish, "It's for me to thank you, not for you to thank me!" We all laughed and went on. But from then on, whenever I saw this old man, he would nod his head at me and smile.

The people seemed very grateful for our work and help. They told us over and over what good people we were to show such love to them. I hope that they saw Jesus and not us. While I was walking down a street the first morning, one lady came to her door and told me that she was thankful for our help. She said, "You do not know how much this is helping us." Later that afternoon some of the officials told us, "This is a great act of love you have come and given to us. We would work with you even if you did not supply food to us, because you have given us hope and inspiration to go on with life." They needed encouragement to see that there was still hope. They still could live normally if they would just get busy and start working.

The size of our village work crew increased daily. The first day there were 50 volunteers, the second day there were 60, the third day 69, and so on. Most worked with a will; small boys of 10 to 15 years worked as hard as the men. When quitting time came, they would race for a big mud puddle and wash their wheelbarrows, shovels and machetes. Every night we put them away, amazingly clean. Then the workers would get their food parcels and go home happy, but tired. As the week went on, we bought three more wheelbarrows and nine pitch forks to add to our necessary tools.

Someone in our group suggested that we should go out to Guatalupe on Sunday and hold a church service in this village. I asked the president, and he said, "Yes, we could use the Catholic Church." (The Catholics are not currently using it.) He was very happy to hear that we wanted to have church for them. So everyone was invited for Sunday morning at 9:00 a.m. Fifty-nine people came. Michael Hofer led the singing, or tried to, that is. We did not have hymn books, so we had to sing from memory. The villagers knew some songs we didn't and vice versa, but finally Michael came up with "I Have Decided to Follow Jesus!" It got a little Pentecostal -- those people really know how to clap! A lady from the village got up and led several songs that we didn't know.

I had the topic, or as we say down there, "preached." We had decided as a group that it should be a salvation message. So I spoke on "What will you do with Jesus?" ending up with the two destinies and the choice we must make.

The people were very attentive, almost as if they were drinking in every work that was spoken. Truly, I believe there is a great need for the gospel to be preached in Honduras.

Following the topic, David Glick and Paul Kauffman had testimonies. After the service, the town sheriff got up and told us that he realized we wanted all the glory to go to God, but he wanted to thank us for our help in helping them re-start their lives.

Monday we were back at it again, but at noon I had to leave the village to catch a plane back to Belize later in the afternoon. I stood at the village entrance saying goodbyes, and I looked once more over the village. I had been there so short a time, but yet it hurt so badly to leave. The people had become a part of me, and I will probably never forget them.

Back at Hummingbird, late that evening, I helped Edwin Birky pack up for his week in Honduras. He left a few hours later at 2 a.m. I left Belize the next day, December 1, for my home in Idaho.

Since I am home, I have learned that the cleanup in the village of Guatalupe is now completed. Now the relief workers are rebuilding houses in an area about two kilometers from El Progreso. In that place 25-30 houses were destroyed, so there is a lot of rebuilding to do. So the Belizean workers going over now will be concentrating more on rebuilding than cleanup.

Some of you may be wondering who is funding this relief work. Christian Aid Ministries is funding a major portion, and also Spanish Lookout has a special fund set up for those who wish to donate funds. Please pray for David Stutzman. He is the director in Belize for the Honduran work. He is a busy man with much responsibility. God bless you all as you pray for the work in Honduras.

She said, "You do not know how much this is helping us." Later that afternoon some of the officials told us, "This is a great act of love you have come and given to us. We would work with you even if you did not supply food to us, because you have given us hope and inspiration to go on with life."

Street scenes in La Lima three weeks after the storm give one an idea of how difficult travel could be in those first several weeks. Even a short walk to a neighbor or the corner store could present quite a challenge. Travel was mostly by foot, four-wheel-drive vehicle or, for the occasional brave soul, a bicycle.

How about trying to keep a house clean with streets like this? That is, of course, if you had already cleaned out the ten inches of mud that was deposited there by the Ulua River and the Chamelecon River. D.S.H.

Rescuers Switch to Feeding and Sheltering Survivors

Reprinted with permission by *USA Today*.

MOROLICA, Honduras–U.S. Air Force Captain Steve Smith settles his Chinook helicopter down near this demolished Honduran town where the people appear as hungry as the animals rooting around in the smashed houses.

Even before the blades stop whirring, hundreds rush towards the chopper that is bringing the first international aid to this town since floods from Hurricane Mitch wiped it off the map last week.

Honduran soldiers bail out first, ready to prevent chaos. Then U.S. airmen form a human chain to unload boxes of food, medicine and clothes for Morolica's 7,000 dazed and drenched survivors.

"This is the worst natural disaster I've ever seen," said Smith, from Burlington, N.C. "I've done search-and-rescue missions in mountains. I've done firefighting. But nothing like this. This is so widespread."

As Smith silences the Chinook's powerful twin blades, 76-year-old Florentina Garcia runs up, tears streaming down her weathered face. "We don't have anything," she cries. "It's all gone."

The relief effort in Honduras has moved full throttle into its second phase: No more plucking people off roofs and treetops - it's time to feed, clothe and protect the hundreds of thousands who survived the worst natural disaster to hit Central America this century.

Nearly 10,000 people, mostly in Honduras and Nicaragua, died in the torrential floods and mudslides. Officials can't even give an accurate death count yet. Thousands are still missing. Millions are homeless.

When Smith first arrived last week from Howard Air Force Base in Panama, he spent his

Even before the blades stop whirring, hundreds rush toward the chopper that is bringing food.

days rescuing people. U.S. forces alone saved 650 people huddling on rooftops or clinging to trees. Honduran forces rescued thousands more.

But it's those that Smith couldn't reach that weigh heavily on his mind. He recalls spotting 100 people from the air Thursday in a little town near a river.

"They were swimming in this soccer field that was still flooded," Smith said. "They were waving to us, screaming. But there was a big power line running across the only small area of dry land anywhere near them. We just couldn't land."

Smith pulls out a picture of his own two children as he tells the story. "You don't know how much I wanted to pick them up," he said. "But I just couldn't." All he could do was radio Honduran officials, who said they would do their best.

U.S. Ambassador to Honduras James Creagan, speaking at the Soto Cano Air Base that is the command center for U.S. relief operations to all of Central America, agrees that the rescue effort has gone beyond saving lives to providing sustenance.

"We've moved to the phase of providing food, food and more food," Creagan said.

He said it is difficult to imagine a country so devastated that its capital is dependent on a fragile air bridge for food.

"It's like Berlin in 1948," he said.

Honduras, already one of the poorest countries in the Western Hemisphere, is now a washed-out patch of island cities. Floods, generated by up to 4 inches of rain an hour for almost a week, destroyed almost 100 major bridges.

It is impossible to drive from the capital, Tegucigalpa, to the country's two major ports or to San Pedro Sula, Honduras' most modern city in the north. It is impossible to drive from point to point anywhere in Honduras.

Government officials estimate the damage to Honduran roads and bridges alone at more than $2 billion -- one-third of the country's gross national product and double its annual budget. That's not even counting the housing and food required for the 1.5 million displaced people -- nearly a quarter of the population.

The only way to navigate the country is by air.

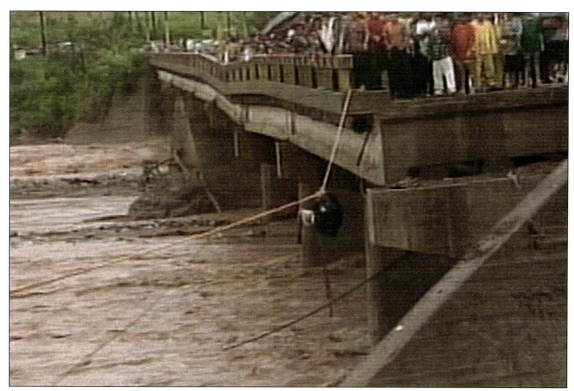

Floods generated by up to four inches of rain an hour for almost a week destroyed almost 100 major bridges.

"They need everything," said U.S. Senior Master Sgt. Jesus Cruz, who helped load up Smiths' Chinook in the capital. "They need food, clothing, shoes and gasoline. They're asking for search dogs to help look for bodies."

Famine in the remote areas is a major concern. Another is disease from contaminated water. In Tegucigalpa alone, 75% of the water supply was destroyed.

Cholera and malaria epidemics could quickly take hold, doctors and aid workers warned. Conjunctivitis, a highly contagious eye infection, diarrhea and skin rashes already are widespread.

Honduran President Carlos Flores said that as aid, which will continue for months, pours in from foreign governments and private charities around the world, he will turn the immediate relief effort to the Roman Catholic Church and private aid organizations to try to stave off corruption. The Honduran government will concentrate on rebuilding its shattered country, Flores said.

U.S. officials will bring in pontoon bridges to get the trucks and cars rolling again.

"We're looking at a quick temporary fix, not a permanent one," said Gen. Charles Wilhelm, commander of the U.S. Southern Command in Miami. He flew into Soto Cano Air Base to plan the United States' next step in the relief effort.

But that's exactly what has many Hondurans and Latin American experts worried. How does Honduras recover when the relief dries up?

"This has been so catastrophic that it's difficult to imagine Honduras ever returning to what it was," said Peter Bell, president of the Atlanta-based Care Relief Group.

"The most difficult part of this catastrophe will come after the spotlight has faded and the mud and slime have receded. The reconstruction will take decades," Bell said.

The devastation to the economy is beyond measure.

Agriculture provides jobs for nearly two-thirds of the Honduran labor force and two-thirds of exports.

But there's nothing left to export.

Bananas are Honduras' second largest export after coffee. But Chiquita Brands International told U.S. officials that its entire banana plantations were wiped out near Tela, along

Agriculture provides jobs for nearly two-thirds of the Honduran labor force and two-thirds of exports. But now there is nothing left to export.

Honduras' northern coast. Dole Food said it lost 70% of its fruit crops in the north, wiping out 25% of its worldwide banana production.

In the end, these companies -- two of the largest employers in Honduras -- may well decide to pull out rather than start over.

A worldwide banana glut could convince Chiquita and Dole that there's simply no point in rebuilding their Honduran plantations. Chiquita already has laid off 7,300 people since the devastation. Dole officials said they are pondering what to do next.

The tourist industry also has been hit hard as Mitch battered the Bay Islands, a popular tourist destination.

One winner in the drama, though, could be the U.S. military. U.S. officials have been negotiating with the Honduran government for 15 years to secure a permanent U.S. military base in this strategic Central American country.

With the scheduled closure of Howard Air Force Base in Panama next year during the U.S. hand-over of the Panama Canal Zone, the need for a new base is even more pressing, U.S. military officials said.

The Honduran government, now in desperate need of cash and aid, may decide the time is right to lease Soto Cano, which would become the southernmost U.S. military installation and the largest in the Western Hemisphere.

The losers, as always, are the poor, of which there are many here.

Maria Medrano, a 17-year-old single mother, sits breast-feeding her 6-week-old baby on a paper-thin foam pad. It serves as a bed for her and her three brothers in a shelter for displaced people in the capital.

"I have no idea how long we'll be here," Medrano said. "Or where we'll go from here."

Many of the country's rich fret that the poor will turn to stealing. A dusk-to-dawn curfew has been slapped on the capital to prevent looting, which, so far, has largely been kept under control.

"Wealthy people are really worried," said Paul Jeffrey, an American aid worker living in a middle-class Tegucigalpa neighborhood.

The losers, as always, are the poor of which there are many here.

500 Aid Containers Stuck At Seaport

Reprinted with permission by *USA Today*.

PUERTO CORTES, Honduras–About 500 containers of humanitarian aid destined for the victims of Hurricane Mitch are sitting in a port in northeastern Honduras.

The millions of pounds of donations came from the USA, Europe and other countries, officials say.

Chiquita Brands Inc. and Dole Food Co. Inc., the two largest multinational fruit companies operating in Honduras, arranged much of the transportation of the containers.

Although the overflow has been reduced from 1,200 containers three weeks ago, progress is slow.

"One of the problems is that many of the shipments have come in the name of a specific person," Port Internal Auditor Benjamin Serpas says. "And that specific person has not come to claim it."

Serpas says Honduran groups in the United States sent many containers full of aid to Manuel Diaz, for example.

"Everyone is named Manuel Diaz here," he says.

Serpas says many international relief organizations in Honduras, such as CARE and Caritas, do not have enough warehouse space to hold the donations until they can be delivered. "The Red Cross only has 45 people working in all of Honduras," he says.

Aid workers say agencies don't have enough vehicles to move the aid that flowed in after Hurricane Mitch struck.

Critics say, however, that Honduran authorities are requiring too much paperwork.

"It's incredible that with all this need, there are warehouses full of stuff," says Blanca Estela Rodriguez, country director for the Kansas City-based Children International relief agency. "The port is full of containers."

Serpas says that although the country is grateful

The millions of pounds of donations came from the U.S.A., Europe, and other countries. Agencies don't have enough vehicles to move the aid that flowed in after Hurricane Mitch struck.

for all the donations it received, too many clothes were sent.

"What we needed is food for the next two months until the harvest," he says. "The people who lost their land don't have anything to eat. They have clothes to wear."

U.S. officials say Americans donated more goods for the victims of Hurricane Mitch than any other disaster in history. The U.S. disaster relief for Hurricane Mitch totals $300 million. Other countries also have sent millions.

"The response to Hurricane Mitch from the United States was simply unprecedented," says Roy Williams, director of the Office of Foreign Disaster Assistance for the U.S. government. "There has never been an outpouring like this. Nothing compares to it."

Storm Leaves Children With Nothing but Desperation

SAN PEDRO SULA, Honduras–As usual in natural disasters, children are paying the highest price for the devastation of Hurricane Mitch.

Hundreds of Honduran children were forced onto the streets when the hurricane cut a swath of destruction across Central America in November.

They are either homeless orphans or are sent there by desperately poor parents.

The kids beg, shine shoes or just roam the streets. Social workers say an increasing number are addicted to glue sniffing. Once that happens, they're lost to the street culture.

Thousands live in overcrowded shelters. They sleep five in a bed and fight over the lone toilet. The only protection from the wind and rain are sheets of plastic. They live on handouts and cook meals on concrete floors.

Unrelenting rain has turned much of Honduras into a breeding ground for disease: Malaria, dengue fever, diarrhea and respiratory problems.

Months after the hurricane has come and gone, some of the hardest-hit towns still are ankle deep in mud. People walk home on wooden planks.

The Honduran economy is in shambles. Thousands of people are without work and have little chance of finding anything. Despite an unprecedented outpouring of aid from the United States and other countries, experts say it will take years for Honduras to recover.

Hundreds of Honduran children were forced onto the street when the hurricane cut a swath of destruction across Central America. They are either homeless, orphans, or are sent there by desperate, poor parents.

Living A Miracle

Printed with permission from *the mennonite*

CENTRAL, NORTH AMERICAN CONTINUE RESPONSE TO MITCH

AKRON, Pa.–Carmen Levia didn't have much. And after Hurricane Mitch caused Nicaragua's Lake Managua to overflow its banks and wash away her home, she has even less.

But on December 10, Levia had just a bit more, thanks to Mennonite Central Committee (MCC) and the agency's supporters. She received one of the first 260 hurricane relief kits distributed by MCC. "I don't feel so alone anymore," says Levia, who now lives in a warehouse and sleeps on plastic sheeting on the cement floor.

"People were overjoyed and surprised by the buckets," says MCC relief worker Jim Hershberger, who helped distribute the kits in villages around Lake Managua. "The soap, toothpaste and towels were items they could use immediately. Most (recipients) are Christian, so they really appreciated the Bibles that were also included."

HELP IN HONDURAS

Honduran Mennonites are helping about 6,000 families, or 30,000 to 40,000 people, mostly by providing food. In San Pedro Sula, MAMA, a ministry of the Honduran Mennonite Church, presents Christian stories, songs and activities plus a snack for the children living in a village of tents in the parking lot of a city stadium. An estimated 2,800 people displaced by Mitch are living on the stadium grounds, and another 2,200 people are expected to join them.

"We're going to give thanks to God this morning," MAMA staff member Lavinio de Ochoa told the children one morning. "Do you know why? Because we were spared."

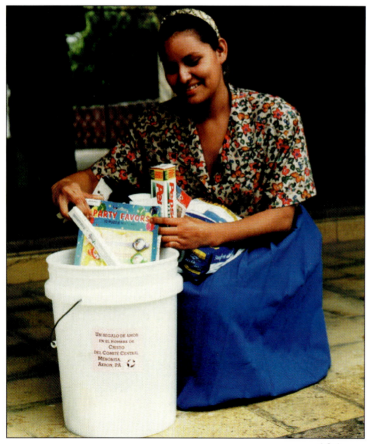

People were overjoyed and surprised by the buckets. This picture of a Honduran lady receiving a bucket shows the joy on her face.

"Si! (yes!)," shouted the children.

MAMA is also helping 600 families in poor neighborhoods in the area and has organized medical help and provided food and cooking utensils. MAMA is also sending volunteer teachers to shelters to work with children who have lost a month or more of school time. With the Honduran Mennonite Church, MAMA hopes to repair 200 homes and build 150 more over the next year. Church staff are planning food-for-work projects to clean homes, streets, health centers and other facilities.

"We are now living that second kind of miracle."

A Honduran Mennonite congregation has donated a block-making machine to one community so people there can begin rebuilding houses. Another congregation served as a temporary health clinic even though it was damaged by flood waters.

Members of the Mennonite colonies in Belize, largely spared Mitch's wrath, have responded to needs in neighboring Honduras with food, fresh water, building supplies and a food-for-work project.

For some Belizian Mennonites, their response is rooted in having survived Hurricane Hattie in 1961. "Since we experienced a hurricane 37 years ago, we still remember what it was like," says Esther Reimre of the Spanish Lookout colony.

FUNDS FOR FARMERS

Meanwhile, 66 Nicaraguan farm families are the first recipients of hurricane reconstruction aid from Mennonite Economic Development Associates. Each family will receive $150 to replace crops destroyed by Mitch. The assistance is part of a $640,000 package of grants and loads MEDA is providing for hurricane victims in Nicaragua.

"It's as if the land was scraped bare by a giant paw," says MEDA president Ben Sprunger following a December visit.

Members of the Mennonite colonies in Belize, largely spared Mitch's wrath, have responded to needs in neighboring Honduras with food, fresh water, building supplies and a food-for-work project.

Stories from David & Nancy Stutzman

Reprinted with permission.

"What really happened here when the inundation came?" I asked the young couple at the small store in the village of Las Ocho. This was four months after the hurricane but the memory was still vivid.

"That large area behind you that is now so flat was acres and acres of bananas and plantain. It had been raining a lot. Suddenly a gush of water came out of the banana field. In about 10 minutes it was swirling around and had reached the second step of our house. We took the children and hurried toward the dike. The rest of the village was going toward the dike too. We all got on the dike and still the water kept rising. We moved to the highest part of the dike. The fields, village, whole plateau was turned into a sea of muddy water. It went two feet over the roof of our house which would be approximately 20 feet deep. We lived on the dike for 15 days until we could return to our house. We had carried no food along so we would swim out and bring in bananas or coconuts that we found floating in the water."

"In 1974 my family was living in Chaloma. Hurricane Fifi brought floods that drowned my mother and father. My brother and I were young boys at home at the time. Since then I moved across the valley to El Progreso, married and built a house near the small creek named El Pelo. Fed by 24 inches of rain in the mountains behind us this small creek turned into a raging torrent. It began eroding away at the banks and one by one the houses toppled in. Between 300-400 houses were washed away in this area. We took our children and left all our possessions which were carried away by the flood. We are renting a house and trying to help our church members that lost everything too."

Along the entrance path to Las Chumbas is a cement block house with a tree near one end. As the flood waters rose the older man living here forsook the house and climbed the tree. Huddled in the tree hour after hour he grew steadily weaker in the constant rain. His calls for help to the rescue boats going nearby went unnoticed. On the fifth day a passing boat spotted him. He was rescued from the tree and carried to a hospital in El Progreso where he died a few days later.

"We heard that the river may overflow but here in La Democracia we have trusted in the large earthen dikes to hold back the might of the great Ulua River during many past floods. About midnight we were awakened by voices crying in the night. As we rose out of bed we found water coming in our houses. We carried out children through the rising waters to the raised highway at the edge of our village. The men returned several times to carry out children, which was now chest deep. We thank God that all our lives were spared."

Approximately one-half mile from the highway is a farming community of Corazal. This village as well as five others are located on former banana plantations. As the waters rose they tried to reach the safety of the highway by crossing the current banana fields going hand over hand on the banana rails. It was hard going and the wet rails were hard to hold onto. Those who lost their grip were swept away by the current. Their bodies were found among the downed banana plants and wrapped around posts 15 days later when the water had subsided. It was a terrible stench that lay over the whole area.

"Now what? Most of our wells are full of mud. Our crops that we were preparing to harvest were completely destroyed. We have no seed to replant. Our clothes and house furnishings are ruined. Our houses are either flattened or coated with mud. We have no food and our employment packing bananas will not begin until June 2000 when the production begins. We sit here with our arms crossed depending on the mercy of God."

As the water began coming into our house, my husband found a place in a tree for our five children and us. I took water and some food. For three days were were in the tree. Their father said he would fix a good place for us with boards then he would throw himself into the water. The children said, "No, no, Daddy, if you go we will follow you." On the third day we heard a boat coming and were so glad we were going to be rescued, I threw away what water we had left in preparation to get into the boat when it arrived. But…the boat was too full. Two days later we were still in the tree when we heard a plane overhead. It came nearer and dropped a small bag of milk. My three-year-old daughter said, "Mama, now we can sing because God is taking care of us!"

Loading a boat with rice, corn and beans on November 11, 1998 at a pier in Puerto Cortez. In the weeks following Hurricane Mitch the only way to access many villages was by water or air. Since air-drops were costly, dangerous and in some cases illegal, water was the only alternative for C.A.M. food distribution. This method, also dangerous at times, was used until other access was found to the villages. The boat shown in this photo made numerous trips from Belize to Puerto Cortez with tons of rice and beans. Smaller boats were then loaded and sent east along the coast to the Ulua River where they could then access the otherwise isolated villages. These boats at times met with rough seas before making it back to port. On one occasion a small skiff was swamped at the river's mouth. Fortunately no one was hurt and only the boat and cargo were lost. D.S.H.

One of the greater challenges for commuters in the aftermath of the storm was traveling in and around the sister cities of Tegucigalpa and Comayaguela. Because many of the bridges connecting the two sides of the river were destroyed, traffic would be bottle-necked at the few remaining bridges. Hence a commute that would normally take minutes could turn into hours.

Part of "tent city" along the highway by El Progreso - La Lima. The first night we were there a baby was born and died in the middle "house" in this photo. They had asked us for help to build a box to bury it in the next day.

Supporters Surpass MCC's Goals for Hurricane Aid

Printed with permission from *the mennonite*

BUT LONG TERM RELIEF WORK REMAINS TO BE DONE.

AKRON, Pa.–From buckets to bucks, North Americans have flooded Mennonite Central Committee (MCC) with assistance as the agency, in response to Hurricane Mitch's devastation in Central America, continues one of its largest relief efforts in recent years.

Supporters have answered MCC's call for 20,000 hurricane relief kits by filling 50,000 kits, and more are arriving daily at MCC offices and warehouses across the continent. The kits include items such as combs, toothbrushes and soap packed into five-gallon buckets.

"This has spilled over to public schools, civic groups, other denominations," says Kevin King, material resources manager. "It's unbelievable."

A Massachusetts plastic company, which found news of MCC's hurricane response on the internet donated 10,000 buckets for the relief kits. MCC's purchase of more than 23,000 Spanish-language Bibles to add to the kits had nearly depleted the American Bible Society's inventory.

"We have been overwhelmed by the generosity of our constituents," says executive director Ronald J.R. Mathies. "The need in Central America is very great. This is one of the largest relief efforts undertaken by MCC in recent years, and we are thankful for the contributions."

MCC is planning for a three- to five-year response, meaning there is still more to do. "We anticipate rebuilding homes destroyed or damaged by Mitch," says overseas director Ray Brubacher. "We also want to help farmers clean debris from their fields and to give them seeds

A Massachusetts's plastic company donated 10,000 buckets for relief kits. Fifty thousand buckets had already been sent by MCC and more are arriving daily at MCC warehouses across the continent. It is unbelievable how people are helping! Picture shows Jim Hershberger handing out buckets in Nicaragua.

and tools so they can again begin growing their own food."

MCC, in conjunction with partners in Honduras and Nicaragua, will be sending work teams to help clean and rebuild. The plan is to send groups of five to eight people from the United States and Canada to work with five to eight Central Americans for two weeks. The schedule calls for sending teams to Honduras each Saturday for the next six to 12 months. Work teams will also go to Nicaragua.

The teams will be expected to pay their own transportation and in-country costs as well as cover their own medical costs and insurance.

THE HOMELESS MAN'S MITE FOR RELIEF WORK

AKRON, Pa.–Mennonite Central Committee's West Coast regional office in Reedley, California recently received a $1 contribution, accompanied by a note from a pastor describing the unique gift.

"Last Sunday a homeless person came to see me," the pastor wrote. "I always try to give some assistance to people in these circumstances, and I take the opportunity to talk to them about someone who may need their help.

"I mentioned that we were helping people in need in Honduras and Nicaragua–people affected by Hurricane Mitch. This immediately touched his heart, because his name was Mitchell. This dollar is his contribution."

A food distribution area. Thousands of people have volunteered monthly to help make this project possible.

Initial clean-up efforts focused on opening main streets and highways. Less-used streets such as this one became storage areas for huge piles of mud and debris until adequate equipment could be brought in for removal. Millions of tons of mud, sand and debris would ultimately need to be moved or disposed of. D.S.H.

The loss is felt most keenly by those who could least afford to lose what they had. Such was the case for many poor who lived along the creeks and rivers of Honduras and received the brunt of Hurricane Mitch. This family, sits among the ruins of what apparently was their home in Tegucigalpa.

Sub Ocean Safety and the Disaster Rescue Brigade

Printed with permission from *Nica News*.

Mission Statement

'The Sub Ocean Safety (SOS) mission is to directly deliver emergency medical aid and relief supplies to victims most heavily impacted by disasters; children, widows and the poor. For SOS, there will be no middlemen between victim and rescue. Our goal is to be the initial response to disasters, standing in the gap between tragedy and the arrival of larger aid efforts.

With advance planning, alert medical teams, a communications database, stockpiled supplies, a logistics bank and specialized transport, SOS will establish the new frontlines of disaster relief at home and abroad.'

SOS History Brief

Likened in the media to the David who faced Goliath, SOS has made history in Central America with its strategies and unbroken string of bold triumphs for the exploited Miskito Indian people of Honduras and Nicaragua.

In 1988, Dr. Beno Marx, Missionary to the Miskito Coast of Honduras, sent out a 'SOS' that his tiny jungle clinic was literally overrun with paralyzed fishery divers; indigenous Indian boys. Exploited by a barbaric lobster diving industry, these uneducated divers had all been victims of paralytic decompression disease, caused by diving too long at too great a depth. Dr. Thomas Millington, answered the distress call, beginning his epic medical investigation into the most brutal abuse in the pages of maritime history. Dr. Millington brought a small decompression chamber (medical science's only tool for treating decompression disease) to Marx's clinic, and the healing began.

Exploited by a barbaric lobster diving industry, these uneducated divers had all been victims of paralytic decompression disease, caused by diving too long at too great a depth.

In 1993, after reading, "A Nation of Half-men," by Dr. Millington, writer Robert Izdepski and his 14-year-old son, Jesse, journeyed into the heart of Mosquitia to document the problem. Izdepski states, "We discovered that there had been thousands of paralyzed divers on this hidden coast. There were paralyzed boys in every village. All of them believed that mermaids had caused their sickness." Faced with the enormity of this abuse and subsequent cover-up, Izdepski met his life's challenge, "All of the disjointed segments of my life suddenly came into sharp focus; I had been equipped to change this evil thing. The sudden realization that I had been chosen long ago, came upon me. I was humbled by the years of preparation I had undergone, beyond my fathoming. All I had to do was be willing to persevere in this trust and all that I lacked would be provided. It has since proven to be true."

Incorporated as a tax-exempt organization in 1994 by Founding Directors, Dr. Thomas Millington and Robert Izdepski, SOS emerged from a thought. With nothing and against all odds, SOS succeeded in establishing two decompression chamber complexes in the most clinically strategic areas of Mosquitia, one in Honduras and one in Nicaragua.

It took five years, but success is sweet. Hundreds of paralyzed boys can now walk again. The entire SOS saga is documented on video. SOS will not forget the incalculable contributions of Susan Izdepski and family, our Board of Directors, Video Producer Jorge Torras, Jonathan Samuels, Erich Izdepski, Dr. Humberto Castro Olayo, Jorge Giraldez-Bernard, David Rossi and Dr. David Youngblood. At no small personal financial cost, these troopers braved hazards and ignored death threats to assist in the SOS battle against cruel exploitation. We were not found to be insufficient.

Today, SOS Disaster Rescue Brigade

With the advent of Hurricane Mitch, SOS discovered the next phase of its purpose. The personal connections we established in Central America coupled with accumulated shipping and logistical experience, enabled us to play a decisive

Robert Izdepski, SOS leader, and his team throwing overboard a four-ton decompression chamber to be transported by canoe up the river to a local clinic for installation.

role in the Hurricane Mitch Relief Efforts.

On Oct. 29, 1998, Robert Izdepski was the first to appear on television news on behalf of the victims of Mitch. While some reporters were still dragging their feet, quoting statistics like, "There have only been six confirmed dead," SOS immediately organized supply drop locations and then arranged shipping for millions of pounds of relief supplies into Honduras.

After the arrival of the first relief ships to Honduras, on Nov. 24 Izdepski flew into the disaster zone to witness the distribution of relief supplies. It was a cumbersome situation, but efforts were slowly starting into motion. Izdepski noted the three-week gap in disaster response.

The next objective was to direct aid to 100,000 Miskito Indians who had been terribly impacted by the floodwaters of Mitch. Being an isolated minority, the Miskito Indians had not received any aid at all. Starvation and disease had set in.

Izdepski located 20,000 pounds of relief supplies, trucked them to the airbase at the capital, unloaded, weighed them and placed them on pallets on the tarmac, ready to go. After five positively certain 'mananas', it was clear that the Honduran government had no intention of helping the 'Indians.' The supplies were moved to the US Air Base at Palmarllo and finally shipped. Then Izdepski went to La Mosquitia to document the disaster.

Traveling with Geoff Mohan, Latin American correspondent for News Day, Izdepski documented the epic flooding in La Mosquitia and the distressing lack of aid sent by the Honduran and Nicaraguan governments. Hunger and disease were everywhere. The river-dwelling Indians had been decimated in the 'lean season' just before harvest time. To make matters worse, all their wells had been contaminated, leading to a deadly epidemic of dysentery. Most of their livestock had drowned. The people were in crisis.

Seeds and Nails

In December, in a Nicaraguan refugee camp on the Rio Coco, Izdepski found malnourished children eating acorns and river-grass soup. There was no help expected. When he asked the village elders what they needed, the answer was

This picture, taken in 1994, shows a La Mosquitia boy milking a cow.

"Seeds and nails." These people are tough, not people who exaggerate their troubles in hopes of a handout. Multiple fresh graves attested to that grim fact.

In January, Izdepski traveled Mosquitia with an investigative team from WWL Channel 4. Three specials were aired the middle of February, and are now up for award considerations.

SOS has arranged for a shallow-draft military landing craft (LCU) to be in New Orleans the end of March, on it's way directly into the Mosquito Coast. Read: NO MIDDLEMEN.

We need HEIRLOOM SEEDS (not hybrid, because they need plants that produce viable seed) for corn, beans, rice tomatoes, squash, and melons. We need 12-penny nails, hammers, handsaws, chainsaws, measuring tapes, hoes, shovels, axes, rope, bleach and machetes. We need over the counter drugs: aspirin, tylenol, cough syrup and especially diarrhea medication. We need money for freight and travel expenses.

In spite of the aid sent to Honduras and Nicaragua, these 'least of peoples' are being left to their own fate. You are the only chance they have left.

Robert Izdepski has just returned from UC Berkley where he was the keynote speaker on this human crisis. He is willing to speak at any gathering.

Louisiana Man Aids Miskitos: Suffering the Bends, Wiped out by Mitch

It was only three days since his return from the Miskito Coast, a strip of rainforested land running through Honduras and Nicaragua, and Bob Izpedski was tired. His weathered face had a pale cast and his voice was strained, the result of 15 days working with storm refugees and fighting the apathy of a local government that seemed not to care whether the Miskito Indians lived or died.

This trip into the rainforests of the region is not the first for Izpedski who, since 1993 under the auspices of Sub Ocean Safety (S.O.S.), has delivered humanitarian aid to the Miskito Indian divers living in Honduras and Nicaragua. Many damage themselves by diving too deeply and

Aerial view of a floating village in the Miskitos Keys, Nicaragua.

rising too quickly to the surface in their search for undersea delicacies.

According to Izpedski, the bends (formation of damaging nitrogen bubbles in the body), if not treated by way of a recompression chamber, can result in paralysis and a slew of other conditions that eventually result in death. As a former commercial diver, Izpedski was stricken with a deep-seated sense that something had to be done.

"As Fourth World members of a Third World country, 90 percent of the Miskito Indian's economy is derived from diving. One in four of those who dive are eventually damaged by the work," he stated. Before Izpedski began offering assistance through S.O.S. the Indians thought their most able young men were being stricken by sea demons. When they found out that the bends existed, and that they are easily avoided the people, according to Izpedski, took to the news "like a duck to water."

In the five years that Izpedski has worked on the behalf of the culturally and geographically isolated Indians, his faith in God has deepened, as has his conviction that faith not expressed through works is not faith at all. Often on a shoestring budget, S.O.S. continues to work with the Indian divers but, after the devastation wrought by Hurricane Mitch in Honduras and Nicaragua, Izpedski expanded the mission of his organization to include the salvaging of that already downtrodden subculture. "They live in one of the most isolated portions of country," he said. "There are no roads leading into their area, the only way in being the navigable waterways."

It was the waterways breaching their banks last November during Hurricane Mitch by, in some cases, 60 feet that has 100,000 Indians displaced and homeless, and another 2,500 missing and presumed dead. "As the flood waters receded," Izpedski said, "along with carcasses of cattle, were large numbers of the dead." Most of the 100,000 refugees found some measure of shelter in neighboring, less-affected communities, but this taxed already strained local resources beyond their limits. "The storm struck at the worst time. It wiped out their harvest and stores of seeds." Essentially, Mitch may have consigned many to a slow death by starvation.

Unfortunately, the Honduran government has responded slowly to the misery of the Miskito

These people are tough, not people who exaggerate their troubles in hopes of a handout.

Indians, allowing, according to Izpedski, relief shipments of as much as 25,000 pounds to sit for three weeks or longer, ostensibly because of an inability to transport the supplies to the needy. Curiously, Izpedski was able to secure transport of the food and medical supplies to the Indians, albeit at great cost to himself, confirming his view that the Honduran government may be using the effects of the hurricane to remove a thorn from its side.

"The Miskito Indians live in rainforests rich in mahogany and other natural resources. Their absence would make it much easier to harvest the area," he claimed. Though his resources and those of S.O.S. are limited, Izpedski hoped to return to the Miskito Coast early this year. But this optimistic timetable is predicated on the funding and supplies he can gather in the United States.

Along with others, Izpedski has worked up detailed plans on how to further aid the Indians and what exactly is needed to get the aid and supplies to them. "Since the only way in is by the rivers and waterways, we have to transport the material by canoe. What we need are two 25-horsepower Yamaha watercraft motors. We'd like to deliver 340,000 pounds of food and supplies so we'll need $10,000 in gas to fuel the boats," he said. Izpedski is confident the supplies, motors, and gas will make their way to S.O.S., but his real hope is for unrestricted access to, and use of, a 110- to 120-man crew boat for supply runs to and from the area.

A problem found by many relief agencies in accepting donated goods and supplies is that some food items perish before reaching the needy. Because of this, and the overwhelming need of the Miskito Indians, Izpedski encourages anyone donating food to contact him first for a list of items most needed.

Other things that are unquestionably needed include antibiotics, vitamins, aspirin and acetaminophen, and basic construction materials and tools, such as hammers, nails, cement, and chain saws the Indians can use, not only to cut the wood for homes, but also to shape the canoe variants they use to navigate their local waterways. Ideally, S.O.S. would be, according to the victims, bypassing governments and agencies.

Bob Izpedski risks health, fortune and the wrath of the Honduran and Nicaraguan

The Miskito Indians live in rainforests rich in mahogany and other natural resources. This is a home of one of the Miskito Indians.

governments in his battle to save the culture, and lives, of the Miskito Indians. The flooding caused by Hurricane Mitch wiped out the homes, crops and food supplies of the Miskito Indians, forcing most into neighboring villages or refugee camps with strained and limited supplies. Starvation and disease among the Miskito Indians, and the possibility of civil unrest, make concerted and timely aid paramount.

The Price of Lobster Thermidor

The life of a Miskito Amerindian lobster-diver off Honduras' Caribbean coast is mostly nasty and often short. Until foreign pressure recently brought some improvements, roughly one diver in four ended paralyzed or dead bringing this prized seafood to richer people's tables.

The centre of the industry—300 boats, and processing plants—is Roatan, in the Bay Islands off Honduras' north coast. But the divers are from Mosquitia, a region of few schools, no paved roads and little else but deep poverty, in the farthest east. They are hired by middlemen, who supply them to the boat captains, almost all non-Miskito. A boat will carry 15-30 of them, each man with his canoe and a young assistant, to the lobster grounds, where—using only ordinary scuba gear—they may dive as deep as 36 meters (120 feet).

A recent one-week visit to divers' clinics run by Moravian Christian missionaries in Ahuas and Cauquira, in Mosquitia, saw three divers brought in for treatment paralyzed with "the bends"–decompression sickness, caused by nitrogen bubbles in the blood, the result of diving too often and coming up too fast. Four more, semi-paralyzed, were being treated in Ahuas's decompression chamber. Two had died. Across the border in Nicaragua, where 3,500 more Miskito divers work, with no specialized clinics at all, seven had recently died in a week.

Not all who get the bends will even reach shore. Captains have been known (a rarity, but it has happened) to throw a paralyzed man overboard. Life is grim for those who survive. Some are bedridden; many who are paralyzed die within a year or two, usually from blood poisoning due to neglected bedsores. Men

Until foreign pressure recently brought some improvements, roughly one diver in four ended paralyzed or dead bringing this prize seafood to richer peoples tables. A Miskito Indian hooked a lobster and is returning to land.

limping on crutches are a common sight. Even the lucky ones will often end a short and gruelling career with at least residual symptoms: ringing in the ears, muscle pains, urinary troubles, quite often impotence.

Why do they take the risk? Money, and good money. Lobster-diving offers the people of Mosquitia by far the best livelihood they can hope for. The area has few paid jobs, and deforestation has led to flooding that may wipe out subsistence crops like beans, as it did last spring. Five thousand Miskitos live entirely off diving.

Their earnings should and could support 50,000 more. They are paid about $2 per pound of lobster–say $4.50 a kilo–and can make over $200 in a two-week diving stint, six months' income for many Hondurans. But much of the money goes on drink, mainly guaro, sugar-cane alcohol. Their families often go hungry and they themselves are often up to their ears in debt, for advances of pay, to the middlemen. So, to earn more, they dive too often and too deep, and pay the price.

Still, there is light in this sorry tale. Four years ago Robert Armington, a former American army intelligence officer, Vietnam veteran and professional diver, came to the area, living in a one-room hut in a diver's village, to train local divers. It was their first formal training in safety or diving techniques. Thanks to him, say doctors, accidents are slightly fewer, and fewer of the victims too damaged to respond to treatment. Mr. Armington has been asked, and is to go, to repeat his work in Nicaragua, after three divers there were saved by Honduran divers trained in his techniques.

Training and, these days, the registration of divers are making things better. So is the recent requirement that lobster-boat captains take a course every year in safety techniques. But problems remain. Overfishing has made it rare by now to find lobsters less than 30 meters down, at the limit of diving safety. And–despite their new training–divers still go down far too often, up to 12 times a day. Equipment is often old and badly maintained. The compressors that fill the diver's air-tanks often lack filters, and air may contain debris. A blockage at depth offers a grim choice: dying suffocated or instant ascent and the bends.

A Miskito Indian approaching a lobster lying in the depths of the ocean. Notice the hook the diver uses to catch lobsters.

139

Dr. Gus Salvador, an American Episcopalian missionary, who treats three or four injured divers a week—with the other of Honduras' only two decompression chambers—at St. Luke's center on Roatan, sees only one real answer: to ban lobster diving entirely. That is unlikely: too many people from the diver up, have too much to lose. Seafood exports, nearly all the the United States, bring Honduras $35m a year.

Yet might the bad conscience of those who eat the lobsters change things? Protests pushed one American importer, Red Lobster, a big seafood chain with over 300 restaurants in the United States and Canada, to declare it would buy only lobsters caught in pots. No doubt it means well. But how can the ruling be enforced? Many of its lobsters, say Miskito villagers, are in fact caught by divers.

If you want to help, please contact SOS (Robert Izdepski) PO Box 834, Lacombe, LA 70445.

Lobster diving boat going out for another catch with Mosquitia Indians on board.

Mosquitia Indians paddling their canoe at sunset.

Record Number of Americans Offering Help

Reprinted with permission by *USA Today*.

MIAMI–Feeling a connection both physical and emotional, Americans in unprecedented numbers are opening their hearts and wallets to a Central America that's devastated by Hurricane Mitch.

This is not some distant war that Americans don't understand, not starvation in an arid desert across the globe.

This is Central America, next-door neighbor and destination for business and pleasure travel, homeland for many of the 30 million Hispanics in the USA.

The sheer scope of the disaster – at least 10,000 dead, more than 15,000 missing, entire villages washed away – has struck a nerve.

"This is probably the most devastating international disaster in a very long time," Nancy Racette of the American Red Cross said.

That agency will spend at least $6 million in the region.

"When people hear of so many who are missing or dead, they feel they must do something to help," Racette said.

The Red Cross logged a record 90,000 calls from people who pledged $3.9 million last week. The agency took 20,000 calls on Hurricane Mitch in just one day, nearly doubling the prior day record set by 11,000 callers after the Oklahoma City bombing in 1995.

Many other charitable organizations are helping, too.

Save the Children will air-freight 560 tons of food this month. Catholic Charities just delivered 10,000 pounds of medicine and emergency supplies, the first such shipment of many more this year.

"These are countries where people didn't have much even before Mitch," Catholic Bishop

Heavy storm damage is seen throughout Honduras.

Thomas Wenski said. "Now the misery index has definitely gone up."

Agencies are being flooded by donations, far more so than for other international incidents.

"Central America is just down the road," said Marge Tsitouris, emergency group director for CARE.

CARE normally spends more than $5 million a year in Honduras, a sum that will be greatly increased for hurricane relief. Normal annual food distribution by CARE of about 4,000 tons will jump to at least 24,000 tons this year for hardest-hit Honduras.

The U.S. government has pledged $70 million in humanitarian aid -- a sum greater than is being spent on other international crises.

About $59 million has gone toward war-torn refugees in Kosovo, Yugoslavia. About $47 million was spent on hurricane-ravaged Haiti and the Dominican Republic. Only Sudan, where millions are starving, has received more from the United States this year -- $110 million.

The devastation in Central America also will warrant the largest U.S. military humanitarian response since troops helped Kurd refugees after Desert Storm, officials said.

More than 1,060 U.S. troops have been sent to the area, mostly to Honduras. The number of U.S. military helicopters in the region will jump from 29 to 39 by week's end.

Officials said both U.S. personnel and aircraft are likely to double, even triple, before the relief effort ends.

"This is going to be a large, large operation over an extended period of time," Defense Department spokesman Lt. Col. Bill Darley said.

While human suffering has spurred the United States to help, politics also enters in.

"This area is very strategically important," Darley said. "We have a vested interest in making sure that people in the Western Hemisphere are prosperous and democratic."

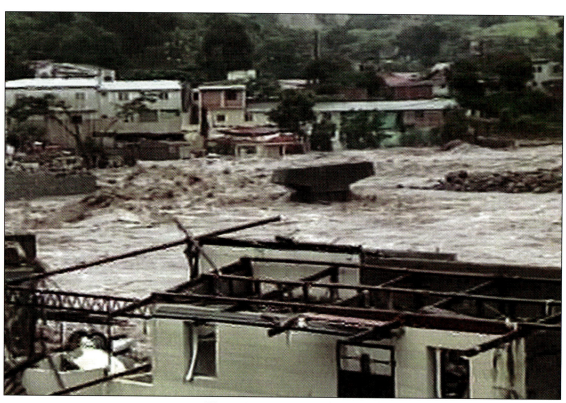

House has its roof missing.

II Sagni Relief Project Conducts Damage Survey in La Mosquitia

Printed with permission from *Honduras This Week*.

JANUARY 9, 1999

The Copan Ruins based La Mosquitia relief project, operating under the name of II Sagni, recently returned from conducting a Damage Assessment Census in the Wampusirpi area of La Mosquitia during the month of December.

Team members: Susan Van der Linden, Angel Rivas de Rosenzweig and Dutch photographer Hiba conducted a census and met with community leaders in the zone.

The village of Wampusirpi is located in the municipality of Wampusirpi, which comprises 18 villages, strung out along the banks of the Patuca River. The region, called the Middle Patuca, stretches from Wampusirpi to Boca de Cuyamel in Olancho.

The zone was hard hit by Hurricane Mitch. Damage reports taken by II Sagni indicate that in the 18 villages of the Municipality of Wampusirpi all villages suffered at least some damage. A brief overview of the Census looks like this; number of affected people 4,617. Number of houses destroyed 182. Number of houses partially damaged 156. Horses killed 36, cows killed 151, pigs killed 311. In terms of agriculture, the zone took a big hit, almost all crops were lost; including 622 mnzs of rice lost, 310 mnzs of yuca, 1036 mnzs of plantain, 492 mnzs of corn and 622 mnzs of cacao (an export crop).

Due to crop loss and the isolation of zone, residents are not totally dependent on outside relief shipments of food. The recovery of agriculture in the area will be hampered by the damage done by flooding, erosion and sand buildup.

During their stay in Wampusirpi, team members travelled via dugout canoe equipped

This shows the homes of the La Mosquitia Indians before the hurricane hit in 1998.

with outboard engines to outlying villages to survey damage.

According to Suzanna Van der Linden; "Upon our arrival in Wampu, much to our surprise we found an organized, Municipal Development Committee functioning."

As to the purpose of the visit Van der Linden stated; "Communications in the zone is not the best, so in order to see the situation and know exactly what type and how much relief supplies to send, we thought it best to invest the time and money to conduct a Damage Assessment Census."

Il Sagni undertook a grassroots fundraising campaign in the US, Canada, Switzerland, Holland, Denmark and England. It has also received valuable support from the North Carolina based, Paramedics for Children, the Virginia based, Central American Relief and Medical Aid and the Tegucigalpa based Tawahka organization, Asang Launa.

Il Sagnis' first shipment of relief supplies, a container of basic foods was sent on Jan 4, Il Sagni team member Angela Rivas de Rosenzweig, a native of Wampusiri accompanied the shipment and documented it's arrival.

Taking advantage of the relief shipment trip. Angela brought in a team of well diggers from Frisco, Colorado. A survey of the Mid-Patuca will be done to choose areas which will most benefit from the well diggers expertise.

Future projects for Il Sagni include; further shipments of basic foods, a short wave radio, gas and oil for outboard motors used to transport relief supplies, an outboard engine to be donated to the municipality, and the elaboration of a long term plan to reconstruct storm damage as well as develop the zone and improve living standards while at the same time protecting the regions natural resources.

We have also heard of other organizations going to La Mosquitia with food, etc.

A typical home of the La Mosquitia Indian.

Forgiving Debt

Printed with permission from *Nica News*.

In response to calls from the Nicaraguan government to nations around the world to forgive the debt owed by this country to them, the governments of the United States, Cuba, Austria, Canada, and France and the European Union have responded positively.

Austria has written off $42 million, Cuba $50.1 million, France $65 million, and the United States $13 million, while the amount forgiven by Canada and the European Union totals $74.5 million. This has effectively reduced Nicaragua's total foreign debt from $6,500,000,000 to $6,225,600,000. Germany and Spain agreed to a restructuring of the debt servicing, according to the Secretariat for Foreign Cooperation, a division of the Ministry of Foreign Affairs of Nicaragua.

Meanwhile, Costa Rican Foreign Minister Roberto Rojas announced in early November that his country "would make some effort to mitigate the debt problem." However, it cannot forgive "even one dollar" because special legislation is needed for this.

Nicaragua owes Costa Rica $480 million.

Minister of Transport and Infrastructure Jaime Bonilla declared that the country will need at least $200 million to repair its roadways and repair bridges destroyed by Hurricane Mitch. Support in the form of equipment is also required. "Not even with all of our equipment and that which the private sector has will it be possible to completely repair the Panamerican Highway, much less the access roads to the municipalities and areas of production," Bonilla stated.

It is urgent for the country to reopen roads to coffee growing zones and banana plantations in order to be able to transport the harvest to the Port of Corinto for export.

On November 11, the Interamerican Development Bank (IDB) arranged with the government to redirect $50 million of already-approved funds for the country to the reconstruction of its basic infrastructure and social projects such as housing construction. The International Monetary Fund (IMF) granted $25 million for this a few days earlier. The World Bank did likewise with $60 million.

We continue to drive over this section of the road for several weeks – even though it had stress cracks going the entire way across the road that were more than three inches wide.

To the Rescue, British Royal Navy in Northeast Nicaragua

Printed with permission from *Nica News*.

NOVEMBER, 1998

The 912 Miskito Indians of Siksayari, deep in the jungle of northeastern Nicaragua, witnessed two apocalyptic scenes in early November.

First the raging Coco River, fed by Hurricane Mitch, swept away their homes, crops and livestock.

Then British forces appeared from the sky.

A few days later, British soldiers and marines working alongside indigenous peasant farmers - with little in common but muscle and good will - had built a half-dozen temporary houses with wood and tin salvaged from amid the mud and debris.

"There was nothing there, everything was lost," said Staff Sgt. Archie Gawl, an army engineer attached to the British warship HMS Ocean.

The helicopter carrier HMS Ocean was on its maiden voyage in the Caribbean when radio distress signals came from Siksayari, a jungle village about 100 miles from the nearest city of Puerto Cabezas in northeast Nicaragua.

The Royal Navy vessel joined the massive international relief campaign that followed Hurricane Mitch, the deadliest Atlantic storm in two centuries.

British helicopters from the Ocean ferried supplies and personnel to devastated villages along the Coco River marking the Nicaragua-Honduras border, waters once sailed by British pirates. Nicaragua's Caribbean region, a former British protectorate, remains largely cut off from the rest of the country in terms of geography and culture.

In Siksayari, a collection of wood houses on stilts with no roads, electricity or telephones, residents huddled in and under the church for six

The water rose fast, giving the people little time to escape.

days, desperately calling out by radio as floodwaters rose around them, before the first helicopter arrived.

"Our brothers here were the first to come," villager leader Nieves Jackson said, pointing to the British troops' muddy campsite next to the church.

Days after their arrival, Jackson was still confused about the origin of the tall, tattooed soldiers in fatigues, mistaking them for Americans.

"It's come full circle…"

"We got a few strange looks from some people, but that changed very, very rapidly," said Willie McMartin, operations leader of the British volunteer International Rescue Corps, which arrived in the region just ahead of the troops. "But in the end the cultural differences, the color differences meant absolutely nothing."

A firefighter from Felkirk, Scotland, McMartin found an amusing irony in the British presence. "Bluebeard used to hide in the Coco River and now British troops are here, so it's come full circle," he said.

In Siksayari, many residents speak only the Miskito Indian language. Few of the British troops spoke Spanish, let alone Miskito. That proved a major impediment at first, especially in providing medical treatment, said Lt. Commander Liz Nichols of the Royal Navy.

But within days, Nicaraguan doctors and nurses fluent in Spanish and Miskito joined the British team in a packed makeshift clinic in the church treating afflictions from malaria, to diarrhea and respiratory infection.

"As you can see, the children are running around here. That's a positive sign, " Nichols said.

No lives were lost to the floods in Siksayari, although illness remained a threat in the aftermath, due mainly to contaminated drinking water.

Residents continued to take water from a muddy stream on the edge of the village.

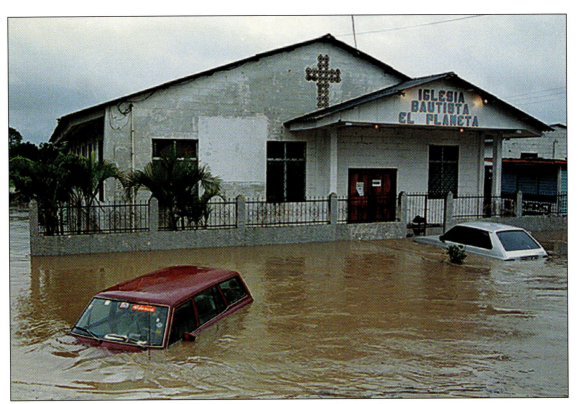

Floodwaters surround this church.

MCC Starts Three-Year, $4.7 Million Response to Hurricane Mitch

Printed with permission from *the mennonite*

AKRON, Pa.–At first, things looked the same to Marlisa Yoder-Bontrager.

"It had been a year and a half since I had been in Honduras, and now I was returning to the country I had grown to love," says Yoder-Bontrager. "You didn't have to go very far before seeing people on the side of the road looking for any place to live. You didn't have to go far before realizing something was terribly wrong."

What was wrong was the devastation left by Hurricane Mitch–the worst hurricane to hit Central America in more than a century. Yoder-Bontrager recently returned to Honduras to assist MCC (Mennonite Central Committee) relief efforts.

Now, MCC workers are putting in overtime to help recovery efforts in Mitch's wake. Focusing on meeting housing and food needs and providing trauma counseling, MCC has started a long-term reconstruction initiative, estimated to last at least three years at a cost of $4.7 million. That's the amount of money the agency received from donors following Mitch.

In addition, MCC has sent more than $3 million in material aid, such as medicine, health and hygiene products, and food. MCC has also received more than 50,000 hurricane relief buckets contributed by North Americans.

"Our goal is to use material aid and cash resources to provide for immediate needs and foster long-term development," says Jim Hershberger, who is coordinating MCC's hurricane relief efforts. "Our partners in Honduras and El Salvador are emphasizing housing reconstruction, while in Nicaragua the emphasis is on food needs, agricultural production and environmental concerns. In Guatemala, MCC is working to establish health-care clinics as well as providing long-term housing."

MCC will spend $1.45 million to rebuild 1,600

Picture showing washed out roads and bridges in Nicaragua.

homes in three years in Honduras plus another 100 homes in El Salvador.

Hershberger said ensuring food security is also a top priority. That includes supplying seeds and agricultural equipment and constructing irrigation systems. MCC plans to finance nearly $1 million in agriculture-related recuperation over the next three years.

CORN BOUND FOR HONDURAS, NOT NORTH KOREA

AKRON, Pa.–After an 11th-hour decision, 40,000 bushels of corn donated by U.S. farmers are on their way to Honduras, not North Korea as originally planned.

Mennonite Central Committee last fall conducted its first corn drive in five years to benefit North Koreans suffering due to a food shortage in that country. But facing a month-long delay in shipping and the expiration of their shipping license, MCC administrators were concerned about the corn spoiling. So they decided to send the grain to Hurricane Mitch victims in Honduras–a much shorter journey than to North Korea.

MCC will keep its commitment to North Korea by purchasing $100,000 worth of beans–a one-month supply–for nursery children in three provinces.

HONDURANS GET TRACTORS FROM MCC

Mennonite Central Committee (MCC) has purchased three tractors to assist hurricane relief efforts in Honduras. The Case IH tractors will be used by the Mennonite Social Action Commission of the Honduran Mennonite Church.

The tractors were purchased at a reduced cost from Binkley & Hurst, a Lititz, Pa., implement dealer. Two of its employees will travel to Honduras in late January to prepare the tractors for use. MCC will pay for the trip while Binkley & Hurst will pay half the employees' salary during their week-long stay.

Mennonite Central Committee is the relief, service and development agency of North American Mennonite and Brethren in Christ Churches. MCC seeks to demonstrate God's love through committed women and men who work among people suffering from poverty and conflict, oppression, and natural disasters.

MCC, Twenty-One S. 12th Street, PO Box 500, Akron, PA 17501. Ph. 717-859-1151.

Man swimming toward rescue boat in street. Water was very deep at this time.

History of Hurricane Mitch

The following is the track information for **Mitch** given in each National Hurricane Center advisory.

ADV	DATE/TIME	LAT	LON	WIND	PRES	STATUS
1	10/22/03Z	12.8N	77.9W	35MPH	1001	T.D. 13
2	10/22/09Z	12.7N	78.5W	35MPH	1001	Tropical depre
3	10/22/15Z	12.0N	78.0W	35MPH	1001	Tropical depre
4	10/22/21Z	11.5N	77.6W	45MPH	1000	T.S. Mitch
5	10/23/03Z	12.3N	77.6N	50MPH	999	Tropical Storm
6	10/23/09Z	13.0N	77.5W	60MPH	997	Tropical Storm
7	10/23/15Z	12.7N	77.9W	60MPH	999	Tropical Storm
8	10/23/21Z	13.0N	78.1W	60MPH	997	Tropical Storm
9	10/24/03Z	13.5N	78.2W	60MPH	997	Tropical Storm
10	10/24/09Z	14.3N	77.7W	90MPH	988	Hurricane - Ca
11	10/24/15Z	14.9N	77.9W	100MPH	987	Hurricane - Ca
11A	10/24/18Z	15.1N	78.0W	100MPH	979	Hurricane
12	10/24/21Z	15.3N	78.2W	105MPH	976	Hurricane
12A	10/25/00Z	15.4N	78.3W	110MPH	973	Hurricane
13	10/25/03Z	15.7N	78.4W	120MPH	965	Hurricane - Ca
13A	10/25/06Z	15.9N	78.9W	125MPH	953	Hurricane
14	10/25/09Z	16.0N	79.2W	125MPH	949	Hurricane
15S	10/25/12Z	16.2N	79.5W	125MPH	945	Hurricane
16	10/25/15Z	16.3N	79.8W	130MPH	942	Hurricane
16A	10/25/18Z	16.4N	80.3W	145MPH	929	Hurricane
17	10/25/21Z	16.6N	80.7W	150MPH	924	Hurricane
17A	10/26/00Z	15.5N	81.4W	150MPH	924	Hurricane
18	10/26/03Z	16.4N	81.7W	150MPH	924	Hurricane
18A	10/26/06Z	16.3N	82.0W	150MPH	922	Hurricane
19	10/26/09Z	16.5N	82.3W	150MPH	923	Hurricane
19A	10/26/12Z	16.6N	82.6W	155MPH	923	Hurricane
20	10/26/15Z	16.7N	92.9W	155MPH	923	Hurricane
20A	10/26/18Z	17.0N	83.2W	170MPH	906	Cat. 5 Hurricane
21	10/26/21Z	17.2N	83.6W	180MPH	905	Hurricane (low
21A	10/27/00Z	17.3N	83.8W	180MPH	906	Hurricane
22	10/27/03Z	17.4N	84.1W	180MPH	906	Hurricane
22A	10/27/06Z	17.4N	84.5W	180MPH	918	Hurricane
23	10/27/09Z	17.4N	84.8W	180MPH	917	Hurricane
23A	10/27/12Z	17.4N	85.2W	180MPH	917	Hurricane
24	10/27/15Z	17.3N	85.0W	165MPH	917	Hurricane
24A	10/27/18Z	16.9N	85.4W	155MPH	928	Hurricane - Ca
25	10/27/21Z	16.8N	85.8W	155MPH	929	Hurricane
25A	10/28/00Z	16.6N	85.6W	150MPH	932	Hurricane
26	10/28/03Z	16.5N	85.6W	140MPH	933	Hurricane
26A	10/28/06Z	16.5N	85.6W	140MPH	933	Hurricane
27	10/28/09Z	16.3N	85.6W	135MPH	942	Hurricane

ADV	DATE/TIME	LAT	LON	WIND	PRES	STATUS
27A	10/28/12Z	16.4N	85.6W	120MPH	949	Hurricane - Ca
28	10/28/15Z	16.4N	85.6W	120MPH	948	Hurricane 28A
28A	10/28/18Z	16.4N	85.6W	120MPH	948	Hurricane
29	10/28/21Z	16.4N	85.9W	115MPH	960	Hurricane
29A	10/29/00Z	16.3N	86.0W	105MPH	966	Hurricane - Ca
30	10/29/03Z	16.3N	86.0W	100MPH	970	Hurricane
30A	10/29/06Z	16.3N	86.0W	100MPH	970	Hurricane
31	10/29/09Z	16.0N	85.9W	85MPH	979	Hurricane - Ca
31A	10/29/12Z	16.0N	85.7W	80MPH	987	Hurricane
32	10/29/15Z	16.0N	85.6W	75MPH	987	Hurricane
32A	10/29/18Z	15.9N	85.6W	75MPH	990	Hurricane
33	10/29/21Z	15.9N	85.8W	60MPH	994	Tropical Storm
33A	10/30/00Z	15.5N	85.8W	60MPH	995	Tropical Storm
34	10/30/03Z	15.5N	85.5W	50MPH	995	Tropical Storm
34A	10/30/06Z	15.4N	85.7W	50MPH	995	Tropical Storm
35	10/30/09Z	15.4N	86.1W	40MPH	996	Tropical Storm
35A	10/30/12Z	15.4N	86.1W	40MPH	997	Tropical Storm
36	10/30/15Z	15.3N	86.2W	40MPH	997	Tropical Storm
36A	10/30/18Z	15.3N	86.5W	40MPH	997	Tropical Storm
37	10/30/21Z	15.1N	86.8W	60MPH	998	Tropical Storm
37A	10/31/00Z	14.5N	87.0W	50MPH	1000	Tropical Storm
38	10/31/03Z	14.4N	87.3W	50MPH	1000	Tropical Storm
38A	10/31/06Z	14.0N	87.0W	50MPH	1000	Tropical Storm
39	10/31/09Z	14.2N	87.9W	40MPH	1000	Tropical Storm
39A	10/31/12Z	14.0N	88.0W	40MPH	1000	Tropical Storm
40	10/31/15Z	14.5N	88.7W	35MPH	1001	Tropical depre.
41	10/31/21Z	14.5N	89.9W	35MPH	1001	Tropical depre.
42	11/01/03Z	14.6N	90.5W	25MPH	1002	Tropical depre.
43	11/01/09Z	15.0N	91.4W	35MPH	1002	Tropical depre.
44	11/01/15Z	14.9N	91.6W	30MPH	1005	Tropical depre.
45	11/01/21Z	15.0N	92.3W	30MPH	1005	Tropical depre.
46	11/03/21Z	19.4N	91.3W	45MPH	997	Regererates
46A	11/04/00Z	20.0N	90.6W	45MPH	997	Tropical Storm
47	11/04/03Z	20.2N	90.2W	40MPH	997	Tropical Storm
47A	11/04/06Z	20.3N	89.9W	40MPH	997	Tropical Storm
48	11/04/09Z	20.8N	89.4W	35MPH	998	Tropical Storm
49	11/04/15Z	21.8N	88.3W	45MPH	998	Tropical Storm
49A	11/04/18Z	23.0N	86.0W	45MPH	993	Tropical Storm
50	11/04/21Z	23.5N	85.8W	45MPH	993	Tropical Storm
50A	11/05/00Z	23.8N	85.4W	45MPH	993	Tropical Storm
51	11/05/03Z	25.3N	84.0W	50MPH	993	Tropical Storm
51A	11/05/06Z	25.4N	83.0W	55MPH	994	Tropical Storm
52	11/05/09Z	25.7N	82.3W	55MPH	993	Tropical Storm
52A	11/05/12Z	26.2N	81.7W	55MPH	993	Tropical Storm
53	11/05/15Z	27.1N	80.2W	65MPH	990	Tropical Storm
53A	11/05/18Z	27.9N	78.8W	65MPH	990	Tropical Storm
54	11/05/21Z	28.2N	76.9W	60MPH	992	Extratopical

Last advisory (11/05/21Z)

CHRISTIAN AID MINISTRIES

Christian Aid Ministries was founded in 1981 as a nonprofit, tax-exempt 501(c) (3) organization. Established to be a trustworthy and efficient channel, CAM enables the church to minister to physical and spiritual needs around the world. CAM sends humanitarian aid and Christian literature into Rumania, the former Soviet Union, Haiti, Nicaragua, Liberia, North Korea and several other countries. CAM also helps rebuild in areas of natural disasters in the USA and other countries. The ultimate goal of CAM is to glorify God and enlarge His kingdom.

CAM is controlled by a seven-member Board of Directors and operated by a three-member Executive Committee. The organizational structure includes an Audit Review Committee, Executive Council, Department Managers, a Ministerial Committee and several Support Committees.

CAM is supported entirely by contributions from concerned individuals and churches (largely Amish and conservative Mennonite) throughout the USA, Canada, Mexico, and a number of other countries.

CAM's international headquarters are in Berlin, Ohio. CAM's meat cannery is in Ephrata, Pennsylvania, next to the 35,000-square-foot warehouse where food parcels are packed and other relief shipments are organized. CAM also operates four clothing centers – located in Indiana, Iowa, Illinois, and Ontario, Canada – where used clothing is received, sorted, and prepared for shipment overseas.

Except for management personnel, most of the work at CAM's warehouses is done by volunteers. In 1992, volunteers at CAM's warehouses, overseas building projects, and at the Disaster Response Services projects donated 129,436 hours.

CAM issues an annual audited financial statement to the entire mailing list. Fund-raising and non-aid administrative expenses are kept as low as possible. In 1992 they were 0.9% of income, including cash and donated articles in kind.

CHRISTIAN AID MINISTRIES
PO Box 360
Dept. Mitch
Berlin, OH 44610
Phone: 330-893-2428
FAX: 330-893-2305

By sending money to Christian Aid Ministries you will be helping these people in Central America to build houses and to buy many of their needs. Please send to the above address and request that your donation is to be used in Central America for the Hurricane Mitch victims.